The Mindsetting Method

A guide to meaningful & productive living.

Written & Created by:
Nia K. N. Jackson

www.StartMindsetting.com

Edited by Darby Baham
Cover Design by Allison Denise of Brand It Beautifully
Valley Stream, New York
Published by Beyond Encouragement LLC, 229-19 Merrick Blvd. Unit 420, Laurelton, NY 11413. For more information: www.beyondencouragement.com

ISBN: 978-0-578-51659-2
Library of Congress Control Number: 2019905853

To those who suffer in silence and are trapped on the battlefield of their minds

The Mindsetting Method

A guide to meaningful & productive living.

1
INTRODUCTION
How did I get here?
Mindset vs. Mindsetting
The Mindsetting Method

2
REBUILD YOUR FOUNDATION
Belief
Your Declaration
Starter Resources

3
RELEASE IT ALL
The Bad
The Useless
The Good

4
RENEW YOURSELF
Your Mind
Daily Thought Work
Weekly Review

5
CONCLUSION
My Results
Your Next Steps
About the Author

PREFACE

I wrote this book to save lives. To ensure that no one else struggles alone like I did for so many years. But most importantly, to show that even the most stagnant and emotionally paralyzed people can create happy and meaningfully productive lives.

Since doing the work outlined in this book, my life has quickly become filled with laughter, growth, happiness, and a future I look forward to living. My relationships are stronger and more fulfilling, I've developed integrity within myself, and I'm continuously building the courage to set boundaries and live my truth. Although these aren't the signs of prosperity that society looks for, they are amazing evidence that I now know my life is worth living.

I had to push through the darkest days of my life to get there though.

On paper, I looked good. Great education, flexible job, fun international travel—all the things an 80's baby is taught to want. But sadness was slowly overcoming me. At first, I didn't know the signs. Eventually things got so bad that the truth of the problem became crystal clear to me. I wasn't living the life I wanted. I had no idea where to begin to change things. And before I knew it, I found myself considering suicide. I didn't really want to die, but I definitely didn't want any more pain and confusion either.

Just when I thought I couldn't take any more pain or stagnation, God saved my life.

Then He showed me The Mindsetting Method that I introduce in this book. By following this process, I've been able to build the meaningful and productive life of my dreams. A life in which I define success and happiness for myself and have the strength to deal with everything else.

As I watch the community of people that look like me and the world beyond it, I see the same pain I've experienced. It's everywhere. Trapped inside that pain are dreamers, creators, and innovators, all trying to figure out how to live their dreams.

The Mindsetting Method will show you how.

1
INTRODUCTION

INTRODUCTION: How Did I Get Here?

A year ago, I didn't believe that I could feel the consistent joy, focus, and balance I feel today. At least not without having any major changes in my life. I thought quitting my job or getting engaged were the only ways to bring a higher level of happiness or a radical new outlook into my life. I'm so glad I was wrong. It is incredibly freeing to know that my legal career, long-term relationship, and prayerfully patient friends didn't directly contribute to creating the blessed life I'm living today.

Although I'm grateful to have a job that pays my bills and very supportive friends, I know they didn't directly create such drastic change in my life. Instead, within three months, I created a life that I eagerly want to greet every day. Forcing myself out of bed in the morning? Struggling through the day at a job I need but don't want? Being afraid that my relationship won't "work" if it doesn't transition into marriage? No, nope, and hell no. None of those things are an issue now. I wake up with joy, move through the day with a powerful and targeted focus, and rest peacefully knowing I can recreate it all again the next day. This is what life is made of: a series of happy moments, learned lessons, and journeys toward achieved goals all strung together all while being willing to grieve the loss of things in between.

So, what did I do to get to this place in my life? Initially I tried every program or tool that seemed reasonable. Then I cried because none of them worked. Then I tried more processes. Even the ones that seemed slightly unreasonable. Then I cried some more because those didn't work either. Finally, I prayed. Not just any prayer. Nothing like what I've prayed before. I prayed a humble, snotty cry, soul-baring, Lord-I-don't-have-no mo', so You better-step-in kind of prayer.

This book was the answer to that prayer. I didn't know it at the time, but in the months before I wrote it, my spirit had shattered. I'd spent over a decade relying on my intellect and the wisdom of the people around me to successfully navigate college, get two advanced degrees, and start my law career. But somehow, I had nothing to show for it. At least nothing that I valued.

The first job I had felt like an intellectual assembly line. Each day, it slowly chipped away at my soul. The second job was an insanely long commute to a black hole of stagnation and lack of procedures. The people at both jobs were strangely ecstatic about having time to fit their lives around their work. And in the meantime, my closest friends were bravely discovering their own definitions of happiness and success. Then there was me.

Every time I tried something, I failed. All my ideas either didn't work or bored me to death. Every attempt to pull myself together fizzled out. The time management strategies I tried weren't sustainable. Most productivity hacks were inefficient when I tried to incorporate them into the rest of my life. Eventually, my mind had nothing left to give. And worse, my heart was numb to it all.

INTRODUCTION: How Did I Get Here?

I was fed up with the lies of the one-size-fits-all life cycle I was taught to believe in. I followed the rules, played fair, and went straight to college. I didn't get pregnant early, and I never got arrested. I did everything "right"! But I still ended up with a life I didn't like. A life I didn't even want. My work and experiences gave me the food, shelter, and safety my body needed but didn't come close to filling my soul.

I just knew there had to be something better than this. What was I missing? Life couldn't only be about education, getting a good job, and working hard. There are thousands of people doing that every day and they don't have shit to show for it. So, what was the truth? How was I going to figure out what a successful life looks like for me? What did I need to do to direct *my* mind toward *my* dreams?

Those were the questions I prayed that God would answer. I was hoping for a simple process that I could repeatedly use to permanently resolve the stagnation, boredom, and sadness I had been feeling for years. I begged Him to keep His response really simple. Make it plain. Crystal clear. Something so direct that I could easily do a good work with it.

And He did just that.

For the first time in my life, I followed the instructions I was given without asking a single question! I had no more fight left in me. My tearfully frustrated existence was proof that I didn't know what else to do. So, I gave it my all because my life really did depend on it.

First, I felt called to get a notebook. Then I was challenged to write down my biggest dreams. Finally, He taught me how to intentionally set my thoughts every day. After a few days, I could see that my life was changing. I quickly discovered realistic solutions for the "problems" I had. Staying positive and happy throughout the day? Light work. Showing up every day in alignment with my dreams and plans? Done! Doing exactly what I needed to do how I needed to do it? Magically consistent. And oddly enough, it was some of the easiest work I've ever done.

Over the course of the next few weeks, I realized so many things by following the steps God was showing me. First, I realized the importance of seeking out and believing in my purpose. For a long time, I thought I only needed intellect and education to create the life I wanted. But the years of stagnation and the unbelievable weight of student loans confirmed that my education wasn't strong enough to power my purpose. I needed to see myself as more than my intellect. I needed to believe in the purpose for me being *alive*. Next, I learned that I needed to let go. I had a lot of physical and mental baggage. Holding onto those things was preventing me from holding onto better things. Finally, I learned that I needed to set my mind on the things I wanted to achieve. Nothing more. Nothing less. Decades of unconsciously thinking thoughts had filled my world with things that I didn't want. Going forward, I would need to choose my thoughts carefully to make sure that they were focused on creating things I do want.

The daily work I was doing quickly confirmed my suspicion that my thoughts and mind, not just my faith, must be renewed daily. Anything left alone in this world eventually evaporates, decays, or turns into mold. The mind is no different.

One day, as I prayerfully thanked God for showing me this process, He asked me to make it my business to share it with you. He wanted me to make sure that you know you're not alone. That there is a way out. You don't have to live your life according to the beliefs and opinions of others. But you *do* have to do the work to establish and direct your own thoughts toward your goals. It's not enough for you to just ask other people what to do. That's like building a house without a foundation. Your thoughts are the foundation of anything you're trying to be, do, or have. So why not build a strong foundation or repair the one you've got? The process God showed me, which I call Mindsetting, will help you do both.

It made sense to introduce The Mindsetting Method with working pages because it requires you to 1) write things down and 2) read it aloud as you review it. I see this book as a self-awareness tool. It will help you build your belief foundation, identify what is and isn't serving you, and direct your thoughts toward your goals. Together, these things will lead you to successfully and efficiently accomplishing your goals.

INTRODUCTION: MINDSET VS MINDSETTING

Over the last decade "mindset" has become the buzz word for all things self-help related. Everyone wants to shift their mindset. Coaches and therapists are telling people that they have the wrong mindset about lots of things. It sounds good when people talk about improving it, getting the right one, or shifting it. But how do you know if you've found the right mindset for you? Is there a signal that tells you when to shift your mindset? Is the mindset that you need different from the one that someone else needs? And how the heck do you consistently keep the right mindset?

Merriam-Webster Dictionary defines mindset (noun) as a mental attitude or inclination; a fixed state of mind; a particular way of thinking; a person's attitude or set of opinions about something. Yet, despite this definition, everyone is searching for the right mindset or the best mindset. Society has morphed this definition into something objective, or worse, something illusive like a golden ticket that's limited in supply. This is all wrong.

Mindset is a perspective. It can't be right or wrong. You don't have to search for a better mindset. The one you already have either serves you or it doesn't. If it doesn't serve you then you need to set your mind on something that does serve you. This is a foundational principle of Mindsetting.

Mindsetting is a verb I created to describe the daily process of intentionally choosing your thoughts and directing them toward your goals. Quite literally, it is you setting your mind on something you want to achieve. The Mindsetting Method is a 3-step continuous improvement process, built on Mindsetting, that guides you to meaningful productivity and success. It teaches you to create a custom perspective that continuously and consistently serves you, not the commercialized, skewed, and sterilized version pop culture has adopted.

I believe Mindsetting is the single most important thing you should do every day. The importance of setting your mind on what you desire is the subject of hundreds of books, movies, and podcasts. Lots of famous, successful, and wealthy people have publicly said that they actively set their thoughts and energy on the experiences and achievements they desire. And they do this *before* they take action. But as much as people talk about it, I've never seen a practical explanation of how the rest of us can do this for ourselves. The Mindsetting Method does just that. If you use this book as the renewable self-awareness tool it is intended to be, you will have no problem Mindsetting yourself toward achieving all your heart's desires.

INTRODUCTION: MINDSETTING METHOD

Society would have us believe that our feelings are super important. That we should make smart decisions after factoring our feelings into our plan of action (see first diagram below). But there's a problem with this approach. Feelings are an unreliable source of guidance. You may have heard the common saying: "Feelings aren't facts." This is so true. But it gets worse. Feelings are fickle. They change so quickly. For some of us, it's hard to keep track of our own feelings! And most importantly, feelings are finite. They always eventually change. They never last forever. If you are making decisions on how to act by primarily considering your feelings, you are making long-term decisions from a short-term viewpoint.

How society says we make things happen:

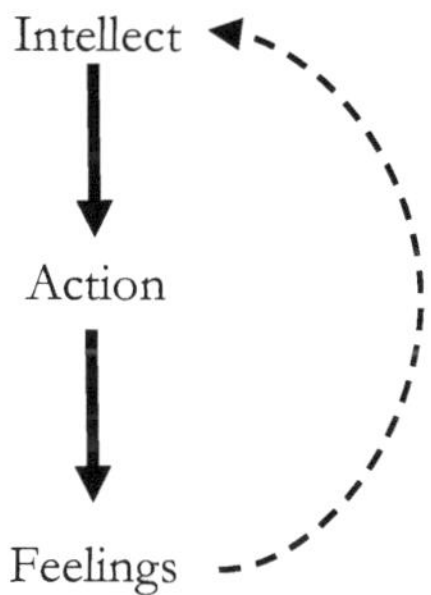

The three steps of the Mindsetting method will improve your ability to continuously make better decisions, direct your thoughts toward your most important goals and take more decisive action. Instead of thinking and acting based on the limited knowledge we have gained over our short lives, Mindsetting teaches us to act on our beliefs—a tried and tested foundation of perspectives that we chose to adopt. With Mindsetting you learn to not rely on the foolish and suspect things we hear and lies we unconsciously infer from our experiences. Mindsetting teaches us, instead, to choose our thoughts based upon the things that we believe and know to be true. All other thoughts must go! This is how you will begin to direct your thoughts toward the things that you want.

How it really works:

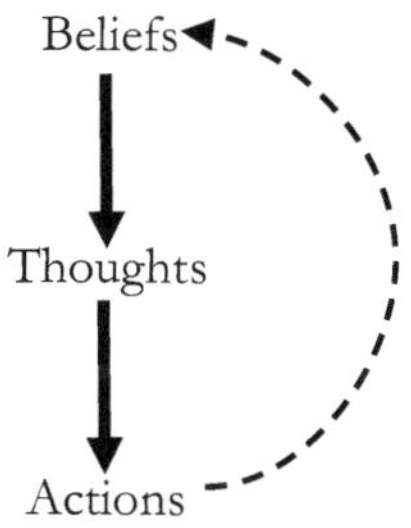

The problem for most of us though is that we can't change what we don't know. You've got to pay attention to what you're thinking. Which thoughts are serving you and which aren't? Once you've determined what you should be thinking, then you must be intentional with thinking it. Every day. Over and over. Without fail.

Between work, family, health, advertisements, foolish friends, and negative influences, there are millions of people and ideas vying for your attention every day. Technology like social media even has a leg up on getting your attention over people because most platforms are structured to pull your attention based on unconscious brain function as opposed to conscious thought. So, don't sleep on the power of all the things vying for your attention because they surely aren't sleeping on you. They work hard to control your mind all day every day. You have to work even harder to maintain control over your mind.

The remainder of this book is divided according to each step of the method: Step 1—Rebuild your belief foundation; Step 2—Release what doesn't serve you, so you can live your dreams and fill your life with more of what does serve you; Step 3—Recharge your thoughts daily. If you're curious about why a certain step is included, feel free to jump ahead and read about it. But please take the time to do the work in the order it's presented and give yourself permission to trust the process.

As you navigate this journey of self-discovery toward meaningful productivity, you will learn a lot of things that will surprise you; but only if you fully commit yourself to the process. The world will begin to unfold right before your eyes in ways you never thought possible. And, although it may scare you at times, if you keep learning, growing, and refining yourself, all the new information you're acquiring will propel you to achieve all that you desire.

Finally, please remember:

1. You are **not** alone.
2. You **do** have the power to change.
3. You **can** have anything and everything you want.

2
REBUILD YOUR FOUNDATION

REBUILD YOUR FOUNDATION: BELIEF

The mind is a battlefield, and what you believe is your only weapon.

I believe we are all part of something bigger and much greater than our individual selves. Not just humanity but a power source from which we can draw information and energy. I also believe that whether you're a Christian, Muslim, agnostic, or science-based believer, nothing matters if you don't believe in yourself. Every dream will be significantly more challenging to achieve if you believe you don't deserve what is available to you.

Many of us build our foundation of belief in ourselves based on the reactions we get from presenting ourselves to the world. This is totally out of order. Instead of evaluating ourselves based on how other people react to us (or might react to us), we must first envision ourselves as who we want to be. Establish the basic principles of our lives and then present ourselves to the world. The reaction that we receive in return should be informational only. It will either tell us something about the people we interact with or give us insight into alternate ways to present ourselves. But their reactions should never cause us to adjust our belief in what we are capable of accomplishing.

Belief is a decision. Yes, even though there may be no supporting evidence, you can still decide to believe in something you don't see. Even if you don't know how it could be possible. Belief still holds power. Your decision to believe in yourself is a notification to the world and your greater power source that you are willing to direct your efforts toward that belief and that you expect great results in return.

You can believe in the power of every religion, science, or energy principle, but if you subconsciously don't believe any of them will work for you—they won't. So, before we can change our thoughts, we must make sure we actually want the beliefs that we currently hold. Then we can make sure our thoughts (and later our actions too!) line up with our beliefs. If you have no beliefs or aren't willing to examine your beliefs, what you should do about a problem is irrelevant.

It's your responsibility to establish your baseline beliefs, which you'll do in the next few pages. Take the time to get clear on what you believe so your thoughts, actions, and all the resources in the universe can work together to manifest your beliefs. I've created a belief declaration to help you get started, and I've left a blank page for you to eventually create your own. As you can tell by now, my Christian faith has been an integral component in my journey. It truly helped me clarify my beliefs. So, I've also compiled a list of Bible scriptures and motivational quotes that you can use to begin believing in yourself. Once you develop your belief declaration, read it aloud every day until it becomes part of your spirit.

WHAT I BELIEVE

- I believe in the power, authority, commandments, and wisdom outlined in The Holy Bible.
- My salvation has already been paid for by Jesus Christ and was sealed by the Holy Spirit. It does not require me to be perfect and it will never be rescinded.
- I have access to God's grace, mercy, favor, joy, and peace every day of my life.
- I am 100% responsible for creating my happiness.
- I belong in every room I enter.
- I deserve to forgive myself.
- There is no limit to what I can accomplish.
- I can be, do, and have anything **if** I give myself permission to grow beyond my current perspective and environment.
- Everything I have experienced can be used to help me change the world.
- If I properly leverage my gifts and the challenges I have faced, I will learn to define success for myself and give others permission to believe that they can do the same.
- I am worthy of receiving everything I desire.
- I'm getting stronger every day.
- I can achieve all my goals and dreams.
- I can do everything it takes to uncover my purpose.
- Society's definition of intellect and success are merely guidelines for the masses and not boundaries outlining my potential.
- I can push past every discouraging word and over every unexpected obstacle.
- Every difficult conversation and challenging situation I experience is an opportunity to learn something new about myself and how I interact with others.
- Being honest, truthful, and transparent with myself regarding love, finances, and my career will always serve me well.

BIBLE VERSES

Refer to these scriptures for help as you start Mindsetting. They were game changers for me.

Why is the Bible my primary reference?
2 Timothy 3:16 (NLT) All scripture is inspired by God and is useful to teach us what is true and to make us realize what is wrong in our lives. It corrects us when we are wrong and teaches us to do what is right.

What should you set your mind on first?
Colossians 3:2 (NKJV) Set your mind on things above, not on things on the earth.

What does faith in God have to do with believing in yourself?
Ephesians 3:20-21 (KJV) Now to Him who is able to do exceedingly abundantly above all that we ask or think, according to the power that works in us, to Him be glory in the church by Christ Jesus to all generations forever and ever. Amen.

What does the Bible say about me having power over my thoughts?
2 Corinthians 10:5 (NLT) We destroy every proud obstacle that keeps people from knowing God. We capture their rebellious thoughts and teach them to obey Christ.

What if you're scared?
Joshua 1:9 (NLT) This is my command—be strong and courageous! Do not be afraid or discouraged. For the Lord your God is with you wherever you go.

Can you tell me what specific things I should be focusing on?
Philippians 4:8 (NLT) And now, dear brothers and sisters, one final thing. Fix your thoughts on what is true, and honorable, and right, and pure, and lovely, and admirable. Think about things that are excellent and worthy of praise.

Why hasn't life gotten any easier since I've started Mindsetting?
2 Corinthians 4:18 (NLT) That is why we never give up. Though our bodies are dying, our spirits are being renewed every day. For our present troubles are small and won't last very long. Yet they produce for us a glory that vastly outweighs them and will last forever! So, we don't look at the troubles we can see now; rather, we fix our gaze on things that cannot be seen. For the things we see now will soon be gone, but the things we cannot see will last forever.

What if I still don't know what to think about?
Proverbs 16:3 (KJV) Commit thy works to the Lord, and thy thoughts shall be established. **Proverbs 3:5-6 (NLT)** Trust in the Lord with all your heart; do not depend on your own understanding. Seek his will in all you do, and he will show you which path to take.

Now that I'm in a good groove with Mindsetting, what else should I be doing?
1 Peter 1:13 (NLT) So prepare your minds for action and exercise self-control.

Did these verses make you get your life? Tell me about it at StartMindsetting.com

MOTIVATIONAL QUOTES

As you start your Mindsetting journey, be sure to seek out new sources of information, motivation, and guidance. Consider all the great thinkers, entrepreneurs, and creators who have worked in your field or overcome challenges like you. But also consider pop culture figures and newsmakers who exemplify personal development and determination. To get you started, here is a list of quotes that helped me leverage The Mindsetting Method and make huge transformational shifts in my personal life and business.

"You are a mind with a body." W. Clement Stone

"Wealth is the product of man's capacity to think." Ayn Rand

"It's pretty hard for the Lord to guide you if you haven't made up your mind which way you want to go." ~Madame C. J. Walker

"Repetition is the mother of knowledge." ~S. B. Fuller

"The circumstances that surrounds a man's life are not important. His response is the ultimate determining factor between success and failure." ~Booker T. Washington

Never stunt your own growth by dismissing something just because it doesn't feel familiar. ~Charlamagne The God

Giving up is not an option. It's a result of not believing in what you're doing. ~Hassan Al Kontar (Syrian refuge stranded in Malaysian airport for 7 months)

If you choose unconsciously, you evolve unconsciously. If you choose consciously, you evolve consciously. ~Gary Zukav

Quit trippin'! ~Steve Harvey

When you change the way you look at things, the things you look at change. ~Wayne Dyer

You'll never know who you can become if you create a life that requires you to pretend you're already comfortable with who you are. ~Sarah Jakes Roberts

If you do what is easy, your life will be hard. But if you do what is hard, your life will be easy. ~Les Brown

HELPFUL BOOKS

To really take your growth to the next level, you will need to dive deeper than verses and quotes can take you. If you fill up on quotes and verses and then stop, you will be just like me when my experiences and education ran out. You will know a lot but not enough. Your transformation is inextricably linked to the success of those who have come before you. Continuing to push yourself to believe in what you can't see will require you to understand the journeys of people who have done just that.

Don't concern yourself with seeking the right answers. Instead ask the best question. As I've incorporated The Mindsetting Method into my life, I've learned that whatever I seek will find me. The books I've listed below have helped me restart my spirit, acquire new perspectives, and have ignited a passion within me to teach the world to do the same.

- ☐ *The Bible* (whichever version you understand)
- ☐ *Start Where You Are* by Chris Gardner
- ☐ *The War of Art* by Steven Pressfield
- ☐ *The Secret* by Rhonda Byrne
- ☐ *Think and Grow Rich* by Napoleon Hill
- ☐ *Year of Yes* by Shonda Rhimes
- ☐ *The Secret to Success* by Eric Thomas, PhD
- ☐ *Think and Grow Rich: A Black Choice* by Dennis Kimbro & Napoleon Hill
- ☐ *Seat of the Soul*, Gary Zukav
- ☐ *Don't Settle for Safe: Embracing the uncomfortable to become unstoppable* by Sarah Jakes Roberts
- ☐ *The Strangest Secret* by Earl Nightingale

Get my newest book recommendations and reviews by signing up for my Book List at StartMindsetting.com.

YOUR BELIEF DECLARATION

In the space below, declare to the world what you believe, and read it aloud frequently.

MY REFERENCE LIST

Use these pages to build your own Mindsetting reference library.

MY REFERENCE LIST

Use these pages to build your own Mindsetting reference library.

3
RELEASE IT ALL

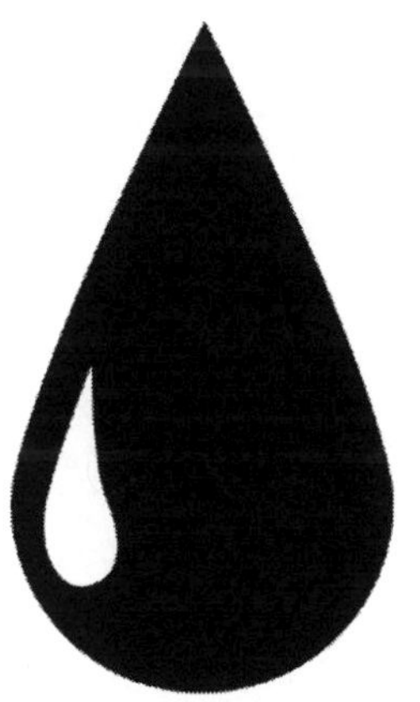

RELEASE IT ALL

All weapons must be cleaned to maintain their accuracy.

If you want to be able to rely on yourself and believe in yourself, you're going to have to work at it. You're going to have to keep the environment of your mind free and clear of clutter, foolishness, and anything that may hurt you.

When was the last time you cleaned your house? If you're anything like me, it gets a decent cleaning every few weeks and at least a quick tidy up every couple of days. So why don't we clean our minds and lives at least just as often as we clean our homes? I think it's because we think (or hope) that people can't tell just how cluttered and confused our minds really are just by looking at us.

It wasn't until I was caring for my father after he was diagnosed with cancer that I realized that this was my truth. Even though I didn't grow up in the same house with him, I had lots of his quirks. Always preferring to give exact change. Trying to "school" anyone ready to learn. Blank cards on deck so I don't have to buy them at the last minute. I thought that was just how I like to be. Wrong! My approach to these situations felt "natural" to me because of genetics. Unfortunately, the rest of my "natural" inclinations and preferences didn't serve me well.

In recent years, I've begun to realize that I inherited and adopted some of the side-effects of trauma, overlooked opportunities, and mismanaged grief. My ability to put my head in the sand and ignore what I perceive to be difficult situations? I know where I learned that skill. My whoa-is-me reaction to being called out on my crap? I see that in family members at every holiday dinner!

For years, I found it easier to ignore my truth than to face tough conversations head-on and risk growing from them. I didn't think anyone could see the emotional baggage I was hiding. Newsflash! Everyone could see it. But instead of running the risk of getting themselves intertwined with such confusion, most people in my life just moved on. I had no choice but to look inward. Everything else seemed like a waste of time. The common thread between all these experiences was me.

It took a long time, but I eventually I made the decision to let my baggage go. I realized that no one could give me permission to see me, but me. We all must work through our own struggles. Even if they were caused by someone else. Your mind is your mess. Only you can clean it up. This section will help you do just that. And it will also keep you from continuously feeling overwhelmed and overworked in the future. Each exercise has a specific purpose: evicting what you don't need, reorganizing what you have, and dreaming about what you will create.

Now, I know you want to bring great things into your life, but first you must make room for them. That dream guy isn't going to introduce himself because you're letting some bozo take up the man space in your life. Your business isn't going to grow because you don't know how to manage the clients you currently have. You must make room for everything you want. With this exercise, I challenge you to aggressively identify all the people, things, and situations in your life that are tied to you staying in the same environment or frame of mind. Be bold, courageous, and don't leave anyone or anything out. You will know you're done when you can say that everything that remains is truthfully hoping for, supporting, and expecting your continuous improvement.

The second exercise will help you reorganize everything that remains after your purge. Now, I'll be honest with you, this is where 'ish got real for me. This is where I learned that I wasn't going to ever have time for building my business if I constantly kept taking on other commitments. I would need to face my truth by lightening my load and relieving myself of some of the burden of making commitments I could never afford to make. This is where you step back and look at your foundation. Choose to spend time on the areas that need repair so you can move forward in confidence.

The third and final exercise of this section is the dusk before dawn. That semi-sleep state where your dreams feel 100% real. This is where you begin to bring them to life. This exercise will help you put yourself, the world, and all the powers you believe in on notice of exactly what you want.

I recommend you do one exercise at a time. Give yourself grace and space to work through each of them unrushed. If you're honest with yourself, your truth will come shining through. And eventually you will see that freeing your environment of people, clutter, and commitments that don't serve you, will make space for elements of the meaningful and productive life you want to live.

Don't keep fighting the same fight.

The signs that people, habits, and situations aren't good for us are all around. I believe they first come in the form of a whisper or gentle nudge. Maybe it's a kind person who cares about you who questions whether you really are loved and safe in that strained relationship. Then, after we don't listen, the sign comes as a stern conversation. This time perhaps it's our job giving us a written warning that if our angry outbursts continue, we will be fired. Finally, if we still haven't resolved our issues then someone or something dies—a relationship ends, job is lost, friendship is broken beyond repair.

I've missed the signs so many times. In high school I went from being Freshman class president to being on academic probation my junior year. Boredom was my excuse. Then in college, I was involved in everything under the sun and didn't listen to my body as it was forever exhausted and rapidly gaining wait. So instead of stepping back I opted for weight loss pills. Eventually, things got really bad and I had a panic attack and almost fainted in my apartment. I was carted through the building where I was an RA by the campus EMTs! So, trust me, I get it. It feels like it comes at you fast, but it doesn't. It just feels that way because you're ignoring all the signs.

Do yourself a favor. Learn how to pay attention. Now is your chance. Successful Mindsetting requires transparency and honesty with yourself. And yes, there is a difference. When prompted you can choose to answer honestly but deciding to be transparent means that you will show your truth whether prompted or not. The Mindsetting Method requires honesty (which I know you can do), but remember, the goal is transparency.

On the next page, name the things that you know have no beneficial purpose in your life. You know, those time draining activities, people, and thoughts that don't truly make you better, happier, smarter or more at peace. If you're like me, you engage in them often, so you shouldn't have to think too hard. Write them down on the next page. You can leave them there to die or you can even tear out the page and ceremonially kill them by burning the page. Safely do whatever you have to do but get those bad things out of your life right away.

RELEASE IT ALL: THE BAD

What I will no longer accept in my life:

Make a list of all the things, people, and experiences that have not served you that you will not allow back into your life. Don't feel compelled to fill the page and don't hesitate to make another page and insert it. What matters is that you write out everything that you will no longer accept.

1. ________________________________
2. ________________________________
3. ________________________________
4. ________________________________
5. ________________________________
6. ________________________________
7. ________________________________
8. ________________________________
9. ________________________________
10. ________________________________
11. ________________________________
12. ________________________________
13. ________________________________
14. ________________________________
15. ________________________________
16. ________________________________
17. ________________________________
18. ________________________________
19. ________________________________
20. ________________________________

Do. Delegate. Discard.

You said you would do it. But you know damn well you shouldn't have said that. Most people pretend to be open with other people, but they lie to themselves every day. Take this time to safely practice being honest with yourself. You are no longer allowed to lie and say you can do things you know you can't do 100% or shouldn't do because of your commitments to yourself.

You cannot pour from an empty vessel. You must learn to make sure that you have what you need, and you are working toward your goals before you commit to doing anything else. In this exercise you are going to dramatically reduce the things that you do by either delegating things to other capable people or discarding the request and giving it back to the person who initially asked you to do it.

So, grab a separate sheet of paper and make a list of all the things you have on your plate. Don't skip anything you owe yourself or anyone else. Nothing is too big or small. Then transfer the tasks on that list to the appropriate section on the next page. Some of the things you will do, others you will delegate, and the rest you will discard.

When you feel challenged, remember that this process is making room for you to build your legacy. This is your chance to stop living life according to everyone else's expectations and rules. There is power in acknowledging your mistakes. Circling back to someone and telling them that you can't complete a task gives them the power to get someone else to help them, while also giving you the power to reclaim time for yourself.

When allocating each task, make sure you consider how much time, energy, and resources you need to live in alignment with the beliefs and personal expectations that you outlined in the previous section. Ideally you want to be able to complete all the tasks you leave for yourself to do within one week. Anything much longer than that, and you will lose your momentum.

RELEASE IT ALL: THE USELESS

Commitments I should not have made:

Of all the tasks you wrote on your scrap paper, divide them into the appropriate section below and execute accordingly.

Do

- ____
- ____
- ____
- ____
- ____
- ____

Delegate

- ____
- ____
- ____
- ____
- ____
- ____

Discard

- ____
- ____
- ____
- ____
- ____

Write the dream. Every single one of them!

Now that you've gotten the bad and useless things out of your life, it's time to release a wave of goodness and prosperity into your life. I used to think that writing out my goals was super important. Then I tried to build a business, sustain a relationship beyond a handful of years, keep a house clean, and look cute consistently. All at the same time. Despite all the knowledge and experiences, I thought I had, none of these goals were easy to achieve. Eventually I realized that all my reasons for achieving the goals weren't compelling enough to make me work hard enough to achieve my goals.

I was told by many that I had accomplished so much in my short life. Trying to achieve more felt like I was ungrateful for the life I had been given. As I began to repair my shattered spirit, I knew this couldn't be true. I refused to believe that I was created to finish all my life goals except marriage and motherhood before I was 30.

So, I chose to focus my thoughts on finding a way to keep achieving. Then I came across, one of many videos by Eric Thomas, PhD. He simply stated that he doesn't believe in setting goals because goals are for self. Instead he chooses to build a legacy.

Dreams and goals are for self. A dream is a mansion or flying international first class. There aren't going to be any consistent late nights of hard work for another house or a first-class flight. Most people aren't going to be able to continuously go the extra mile for material things or short-term experiences. Achievement beyond meeting your basic needs or material wants is going to require that you have a clear legacy vision.

Your legacy may give you tokens of enjoyment, but it's much bigger than that. Your legacy benefits everyone else including your family, community, country, and the world. Having a legacy will allow you to have an impact beyond your life. It will compel you to go the extra mile. It is your reason for doing everything that you do the way that only you can. So, on the next few pages, tell yourself and the Universe how you plan to leave an impact on this world by writing out the components of your legacy on the next few pages.

You can't run from it, hide from it, and still become it.
~Bishop T. D. Jakes

Economic Legacy

Try to blow your own mind by writing the vision of the financial and economic milestones you will hit in your future.

1. ______________________________
2. ______________________________
3. ______________________________
4. ______________________________
5. ______________________________
6. ______________________________
7. ______________________________
8. ______________________________
9. ______________________________
10. ______________________________
11. ______________________________
12. ______________________________
13. ______________________________
14. ______________________________
15. ______________________________
16. ______________________________
17. ______________________________
18. ______________________________
19. ______________________________
20. ______________________________

Personal Development Legacy

List all the concepts you envision yourself learning, new perspectives you will acquire, and problems you will resolve as part of your legacy. Take a shot at filling the page!

1. __________
2. __________
3. __________
4. __________
5. __________
6. __________
7. __________
8. __________
9. __________
10. __________
11. __________
12. __________
13. __________
14. __________
15. __________
16. __________
17. __________
18. __________
19. __________
20. __________

Business Legacy

List out the ways you will transform lives, leave an impact, and amplify the mission of your business.

1. ____________________
2. ____________________
3. ____________________
4. ____________________
5. ____________________
6. ____________________
7. ____________________
8. ____________________
9. ____________________
10. ____________________
11. ____________________
12. ____________________
13. ____________________
14. ____________________
15. ____________________
16. ____________________
17. ____________________
18. ____________________
19. ____________________
20. ____________________

Notes

4
RENEW YOURSELF

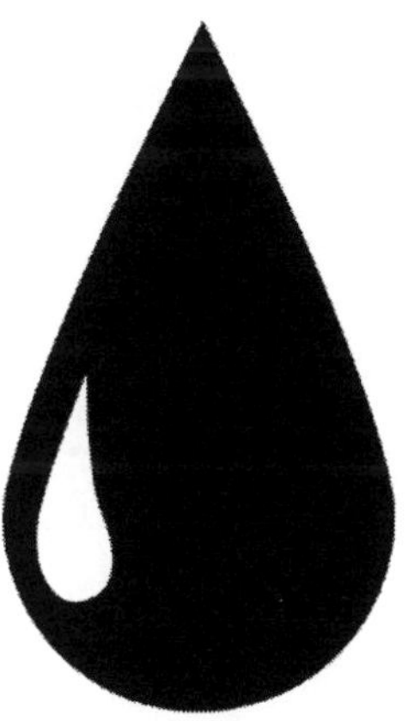

What you believe is your weapon, and your thoughts are your ammunition.

The change you want to see begins with your thoughts. This is where your changed self is carved out of the stone of the foundation you've built through the exercises in the previous sections. Unfortunately, for many of us, our thoughts are on a negative loop. We think thoughts like: "I hope nothing bad happens." "I'm always forgetting things." "I don't want to be alone." These types of thoughts are why we're stuck. And this isn't the bad news. The bad news is that, even if our thoughts are positive, they are usually at a very low-expectation level. This is almost as bad as purely negative thoughts.

Low expectation thinking gives the false security of technically thinking positive thoughts while also believing that you aren't worthy of whatever you desire. We all know that we should try to declutter our minds, stop thinking bad thoughts, and shift our perspectives. But, none of that will work if we aren't clear about what we do want to think about or have in our minds. To successfully stop doing something you must replace that action with a different action.

I once read a powerful quote by Peter Drucker, an acclaimed businessman and strategist: "There is nothing so useless as doing efficiently that which should not be done at all." The power of that quote stayed with me for quite a while until I saw the power of The Mindsetting Method in my own life. The changes in me ran shockingly deep. I literally feel like a reset button has been pressed. The joy, contentment, and happiness that I feel is not just an outlook. It's truly in my spirit. And it's all because I decided to and have continuously set my mind solely toward the achievements and experiences I want to have.

Eventually, when I re-considered that quote, I said to myself: There is nothing so detrimental as thinking repeatedly a thought that should have never been chosen. Yes chosen. I know you don't think you can control your thoughts. But the truth is—you can. Thinking is just as much proactive as it is reactive. Just because a thought comes to you doesn't mean you have to let it stay. If you aren't who you want to be or don't have what you want to have, you need to change your thoughts. It's just that simple. Everything that has ever been done or created in this world began with a thought. The key to success, happiness, peace, and growth is all the same. You must manage your thoughts.

The daily thought work part of The Mindsetting Method is much like building a house. All houses, whether shacks, mansions, or cabins in the woods have the same basic components: a foundation, four walls, and a roof. The differences between each house are mostly in the architectural style and décor. It's your job to choose thoughts that support you in building the life and legacy that you want. Every day, you need to direct your thoughts toward your legacy. Read the prompts on the next few pages. Then, on the daily pages, fill in your response to each prompt every morning and night. Finally, review your entries at the end of each week by reading them out loud. I've provided you with three months of working pages so you can fully integrate The Mindsetting Method into your life.

RENEW YOURSELF: DAILY STEPS

Morning Work

1. **Higher Beliefs Reminder** (Foundation): Write down a Memory Bible Verse or Memory Quote that will remind you that you don't have to go through any day alone. God and all the great thinkers who have gone before you are with you always.
   Example: 1 Peter 1:13 (NLT) So prepare your mind for action and exercise self-control.

2. **Gratitude** (Walls): Start your day with gratitude. Thank the higher power that you believe in. Show thanks for things that you believe are coming not just the things that you have already received. Build up an energy of appreciation and gratefulness that will surround you throughout the day. Bullet points, numbered lists, or full sentences; it doesn't matter. Just say thanks.
   Example: I'm so grateful for friends and family that support me even when they don't understand my ideas.

3. **Daily Declaration** (Bring good energy into the house): Declare just how wonderful your day is going to be. Tell yourself how you are going to show up in the world today. First you must think it, then you can make it so. In a short but specific sentence, put into motion how effective, kind, and focused you are going to be today.
   Example: Today will be productive, efficient, intentional, and calm.

4. **Future Focus** (Roof): What does your future self need your current self to do today? What do you need to improve or change to become the person you want to be in the future? What do you need to learn today so your future self can manage all the great things coming to you?
   Example: My future self needs my current self to learn to be on time so that my future self will be reliable in business.

5. **Purposeful Priority** (Kitchen): Do you have every appliance you own on your countertop? That's a confusing and cluttered way to operate and it's wasteful. Who has time to move things around so you can use one appliance? This prompt is to help you express how you're going to show up today so that you can act in alignment with your beliefs. Take time to set and remind yourself of your only priority, which should be purposeful. Not tasks. Not goals. A singular purpose.
   Example: Do all things with a 1 Corinthians 10:31 spirit.

Night Work

6. **Recap & Redo** (Bathroom): Take the time to think through your thoughts, actions, and reactions to everything that happened today. When you remember something that you wished you handled differently, take the time to actually speak out loud or physically do that action differently. It should almost feel like a replay, but better. Practicing a different action or reaction will condition your mind and body to make a different choice. This will ensure that you are prepared for when the situation comes up again. Cause let's face it, if you didn't handle something or someone properly, the Universe is going to graciously give you another chance to learn your lesson.
   Example: Today was great for productivity and focus. If I could re-do anything, I would get up earlier so I could finish my work and still be on time.

7. **Gratitude** (More Walls): Close out your day with more gratitude for what happened today and for what is to come. This is like shutting and locking your front door at night. You did it this morning and you've got to do it again tonight, but it keeps you and what you care about safe.
   Example: I'm grateful for noticing evidence of exactly what I need right after I detected a problem so I can quickly resolve it. I look forward to being able to see more solutions than problems in the future.

8. **Night Vision** (Circulate more good energy around the house): Take time to carry a specific vision or prayer with you to bed. Use this time to envision whatever or whoever you want to draw to your life. Fall asleep thinking of all the phenomenal things you want to bring to your reality tomorrow.
   Example: I look forward to increasing my physical health and having the wisdom to make the best decisions for my body.

RENEW YOURSELF: DAILY THOUGHT WORK

Date______________

Memory Verse/Memory Quote ____

____

____

____

Morning Gratitude____

____

____

____

____

____

____

____

____

____

Daily Declaration Today I declare that my day will be ______________________

____

____

____

Future Focus My future self needs my current self to ______________________

________________________________ so that my future self will be able to ______

____

____

____

Purposeful Priority To ensure that I remain in alignment with my purpose, my number one priority today is to show up with a spirit of ______________________________

____

____

____

____

____

Recap & Re-do ____

____

____

____

____

____

____

____

____

____

Evening Gratitude ____

____

____

____

____

____

____

____

____

____

____

____

____

Night Vision ____

____

____

____

____

____

____

RENEW YOURSELF: DAILY THOUGHT WORK

Date______________

Memory Verse/Memory Quote ____

____

____

____

Morning Gratitude____

____

____

____

____

____

____

____

____

____

Daily Declaration Today I declare that my day will be ______________________

____

____

____

Future Focus My future self needs my current self to ______________________

________________________________ so that my future self will be able to ______

____

____

____

Purposeful Priority To ensure that I remain in alignment with my purpose, my number one priority today is to show up with a spirit of ______________________________

____

____

____

____

____

Recap & Re-do

Evening Gratitude

Night Vision

Date______________

Memory Verse/Memory Quote ____

____

____

____

Morning Gratitude____

____

____

____

____

____

____

____

____

____

Daily Declaration Today I declare that my day will be ____________________

____

____

____

Future Focus My future self needs my current self to ______________________

______________________________ so that my future self will be able to ______

____

____

____

Purposeful Priority To ensure that I remain in alignment with my purpose, my number one priority today is to show up with a spirit of ____________________________

____

____

____

____

____

Recap & Re-do ____

____

____

____

____

____

____

____

____

____

Evening Gratitude ____

____

____

____

____

____

____

____

____

____

____

____

____

Night Vision ____

____

____

____

____

____

____

RENEW YOURSELF: DAILY THOUGHT WORK

Date______________

Memory Verse/Memory Quote ____

____

____

____

Morning Gratitude____

____

____

____

____

____

____

____

____

____

Daily Declaration Today I declare that my day will be _______________________

____

____

____

Future Focus My future self needs my current self to _______________________

______________________________ so that my future self will be able to ______

____

____

____

Purposeful Priority To ensure that I remain in alignment with my purpose, my number one priority today is to show up with a spirit of ____________________________

____

____

____

____

____

Recap & Re-do ____

____

____

____

____

____

____

____

____

____

Evening Gratitude ____

____

____

____

____

____

____

____

____

____

____

____

____

Night Vision ____

____

____

____

____

____

____

RENEW YOURSELF: DAILY THOUGHT WORK

Date______________

Memory Verse/Memory Quote ____

Morning Gratitude____

Daily Declaration Today I declare that my day will be ______________________

Future Focus My future self needs my current self to ______________________

________________________________ so that my future self will be able to ______

Purposeful Priority To ensure that I remain in alignment with my purpose, my number one priority today is to show up with a spirit of ______________________________

Recap & Re-do ______________________________

Evening Gratitude ______________________________

Night Vision ______________________________

RENEW YOURSELF: DAILY THOUGHT WORK

Date______________

Memory Verse/Memory Quote ____

____

____

____

Morning Gratitude____

____

____

____

____

____

____

____

____

____

Daily Declaration Today I declare that my day will be ______________________

____

____

____

Future Focus My future self needs my current self to ______________________

______________________________ so that my future self will be able to ______

____

____

____

Purposeful Priority To ensure that I remain in alignment with my purpose, my number one priority today is to show up with a spirit of ____________________________

____

____

____

____

____

Recap & Re-do ____________________

Evening Gratitude ____________________

Night Vision ____________________

RENEW YOURSELF: DAILY THOUGHT WORK

Date______________

Memory Verse/Memory Quote ____

____

____

____

Morning Gratitude____

____

____

____

____

____

____

____

____

____

Daily Declaration Today I declare that my day will be ______________________

____

____

____

Future Focus My future self needs my current self to ______________________

________________________________ so that my future self will be able to ______

____

____

____

Purposeful Priority To ensure that I remain in alignment with my purpose, my number one priority today is to show up with a spirit of ____________________________

____

____

____

____

____

Recap & Re-do ______________________________

Evening Gratitude ______________________________

Night Vision ______________________________

RENEW YOURSELF: WEEKLY REVIEW

Date ________________

BELIEF ASSESSMENT

Take this time to infer what your thoughts and gratitude say about your beliefs.

What do my thoughts show I believe in? ________________________________

____

____

____

____

What am I reading to develop, expand, or change my beliefs? ________________

____

____

____

____

____

MENTAL FOCUS ASSESSMENT

What things was I focused on this past week?

________________	________________
________________	________________
________________	________________
________________	________________
________________	________________
________________	________________
________________	________________
________________	________________

RENEW YOURSELF: WEEKLY REVIEW

Of these things, which are a necessary resource, task, or belief that I need to create the life I'm trying to build? Which are not?

NECESSARY	NOT NECESSARY
______________________________	______________________________
______________________________	______________________________
______________________________	______________________________
______________________________	______________________________
______________________________	______________________________
______________________________	______________________________

Why did I choose to focus on the things in the not necessary column? What am I going to do to make sure I don't waste time on these things going forward?____________

____

____

____

____

ACTIONS

What actions were in alignment with my beliefs and a result of my focus? ________

____

____

What actions were not in alignment with my beliefs?________________________

____

____

How can I make my actions align with my beliefs? __________________________

____

RENEW YOURSELF: DAILY THOUGHT WORK

Date______________

Memory Verse/Memory Quote ____

____

____

____

Morning Gratitude____

____

____

____

____

____

____

____

____

____

Daily Declaration Today I declare that my day will be ______________________

____

____

____

Future Focus My future self needs my current self to _______________________

________________________________ so that my future self will be able to ______

____

____

____

Purposeful Priority To ensure that I remain in alignment with my purpose, my number one priority today is to show up with a spirit of ______________________________

____

____

____

____

____

Recap & Re-do ______________________________

Evening Gratitude ______________________________

Night Vision ______________________________

RENEW YOURSELF: DAILY THOUGHT WORK

Date______________

Memory Verse/Memory Quote ____

____

____

____

Morning Gratitude____

____

____

____

____

____

____

____

____

____

Daily Declaration Today I declare that my day will be ____________________

____

____

____

Future Focus My future self needs my current self to ____________________

______________________________ so that my future self will be able to ______

____

____

____

Purposeful Priority To ensure that I remain in alignment with my purpose, my number one priority today is to show up with a spirit of ____________________

____

____

____

____

____

Recap & Re-do ____

Evening Gratitude ____

Night Vision ____

RENEW YOURSELF: DAILY THOUGHT WORK

Date______________

Memory Verse/Memory Quote ____

____

____

____

Morning Gratitude____

____

____

____

____

____

____

____

____

____

Daily Declaration Today I declare that my day will be ______________________

____

____

____

Future Focus My future self needs my current self to _____________________

________________________________ so that my future self will be able to ______

____

____

____

Purposeful Priority To ensure that I remain in alignment with my purpose, my number one priority today is to show up with a spirit of ___________________________

____

____

____

____

____

Recap & Re-do ______________________________

Evening Gratitude ______________________________

Night Vision ______________________________

RENEW YOURSELF: DAILY THOUGHT WORK

Date______________

Memory Verse/Memory Quote ____

____

____

____

Morning Gratitude____

____

____

____

____

____

____

____

____

____

Daily Declaration Today I declare that my day will be ____________________

____

____

____

Future Focus My future self needs my current self to ____________________

______________________________ so that my future self will be able to ______

____

____

____

Purposeful Priority To ensure that I remain in alignment with my purpose, my number one priority today is to show up with a spirit of ____________________________

____

____

____

____

____

Recap & Re-do ______________________________

Evening Gratitude ______________________________

Night Vision ______________________________

RENEW YOURSELF: DAILY THOUGHT WORK

Date_______________

Memory Verse/Memory Quote ____

Morning Gratitude____

Daily Declaration Today I declare that my day will be _________________________

Future Focus My future self needs my current self to ____________________________ _____________________________________ so that my future self will be able to ______

Purposeful Priority To ensure that I remain in alignment with my purpose, my number one priority today is to show up with a spirit of _________________________________

Recap & Re-do ______________________________

____

____

____

____

____

____

____

____

____

Evening Gratitude ______________________________

____

____

____

____

____

____

____

____

____

____

____

____

Night Vision ______________________________

____

____

____

____

____

____

RENEW YOURSELF: DAILY THOUGHT WORK

Date______________

Memory Verse/Memory Quote ____

____

____

____

Morning Gratitude____

____

____

____

____

____

____

____

____

____

Daily Declaration Today I declare that my day will be ________________________

____

____

____

Future Focus My future self needs my current self to ________________________

________________________________ so that my future self will be able to ______

____

____

____

Purposeful Priority To ensure that I remain in alignment with my purpose, my number one priority today is to show up with a spirit of ______________________________

____

____

____

____

____

Recap & Re-do ______________________________

Evening Gratitude ______________________________

Night Vision ______________________________

RENEW YOURSELF: DAILY THOUGHT WORK

Date______________

Memory Verse/Memory Quote ____

____

____

____

Morning Gratitude____

____

____

____

____

____

____

____

____

____

Daily Declaration Today I declare that my day will be ________________________

____

____

____

Future Focus My future self needs my current self to ________________________

________________________________ so that my future self will be able to ______

____

____

____

Purposeful Priority To ensure that I remain in alignment with my purpose, my number one priority today is to show up with a spirit of ______________________________

____

____

____

____

____

Recap & Re-do ______________________________

Evening Gratitude ______________________________

Night Vision ______________________________

RENEW YOURSELF: WEEKLY REVIEW

Date ________________

BELIEF ASSESSMENT

Take this time to infer what your thoughts and gratitude say about your beliefs.

What do my thoughts show I believe in? ________________________________

____

____

____

____

What am I reading to develop, expand, or change my beliefs? ________________

____

____

____

____

____

MENTAL FOCUS ASSESSMENT

What things was I focused on this past week?

______________________________ ______________________________

______________________________ ______________________________

______________________________ ______________________________

______________________________ ______________________________

______________________________ ______________________________

______________________________ ______________________________

______________________________ ______________________________

______________________________ ______________________________

______________________________ ______________________________

RENEW YOURSELF: WEEKLY REVIEW

Of these things, which are a necessary resource, task, or belief that I need to create the life I'm trying to build? Which are not?

NECESSARY	NOT NECESSARY
______________________________	______________________________
______________________________	______________________________
______________________________	______________________________
______________________________	______________________________
______________________________	______________________________
______________________________	______________________________

Why did I choose to focus on the things in the not necessary column? What am I going to do to make sure I don't waste time on these things going forward?____________

____

____

____

____

ACTIONS

What actions were in alignment with my beliefs and a result of my focus? ________

____

____

What actions were not in alignment with my beliefs?________________________

____

____

How can I make my actions align with my beliefs? _________________________

____

____

RENEW YOURSELF: DAILY THOUGHT WORK

Date_____________

Memory Verse/Memory Quote ____

____

____

____

Morning Gratitude____

____

____

____

____

____

____

____

____

____

Daily Declaration Today I declare that my day will be ______________________

____

____

____

Future Focus My future self needs my current self to ______________________

______________________________ so that my future self will be able to ______

____

____

____

Purposeful Priority To ensure that I remain in alignment with my purpose, my number one priority today is to show up with a spirit of ____________________________

____

____

____

____

____

Recap & Re-do ______________________________

Evening Gratitude ______________________________

Night Vision ______________________________

RENEW YOURSELF: DAILY THOUGHT WORK

Date______________

Memory Verse/Memory Quote ____

____

____

____

Morning Gratitude____

____

____

____

____

____

____

____

____

____

Daily Declaration Today I declare that my day will be ______________________

____

____

____

Future Focus My future self needs my current self to ______________________

________________________________ so that my future self will be able to ______

____

____

____

Purposeful Priority To ensure that I remain in alignment with my purpose, my number one priority today is to show up with a spirit of ______________________________

____

____

____

____

____

Recap & Re-do ______________________________

Evening Gratitude ______________________________

Night Vision ______________________________

RENEW YOURSELF: DAILY THOUGHT WORK

Date______________

Memory Verse/Memory Quote ____

____

____

____

Morning Gratitude____

____

____

____

____

____

____

____

____

____

Daily Declaration Today I declare that my day will be _______________________

____

____

____

Future Focus My future self needs my current self to ________________________
_______________________________ so that my future self will be able to ______

____

____

____

Purposeful Priority To ensure that I remain in alignment with my purpose, my number one priority today is to show up with a spirit of ____________________________

____

____

____

____

____

Recap & Re-do ____________________

Evening Gratitude ____________________

Night Vision ____________________

RENEW YOURSELF: DAILY THOUGHT WORK

Date______________

Memory Verse/Memory Quote ____

____

____

____

Morning Gratitude____

____

____

____

____

____

____

____

____

____

Daily Declaration Today I declare that my day will be _______________________

____

____

____

Future Focus My future self needs my current self to _______________________

________________________________ so that my future self will be able to ______

____

____

____

Purposeful Priority To ensure that I remain in alignment with my purpose, my number one priority today is to show up with a spirit of ___________________________

____

____

____

____

____

Recap & Re-do ______________________________

____
____
____
____
____
____
____
____
____

Evening Gratitude ______________________________

____
____
____
____
____
____
____
____
____
____
____
____

Night Vision ______________________________

____
____
____
____
____
____

RENEW YOURSELF: DAILY THOUGHT WORK

Date______________

Memory Verse/Memory Quote ____

____

____

____

Morning Gratitude____

____

____

____

____

____

____

____

____

____

Daily Declaration Today I declare that my day will be _______________________

____

____

____

Future Focus My future self needs my current self to _______________________

_______________________________ so that my future self will be able to ______

____

____

____

Purposeful Priority To ensure that I remain in alignment with my purpose, my number one priority today is to show up with a spirit of ______________________________

____

____

____

____

____

Recap & Re-do

Evening Gratitude

Night Vision

RENEW YOURSELF: DAILY THOUGHT WORK

Date______________

Memory Verse/Memory Quote ____

____

____

____

Morning Gratitude____

____

____

____

____

____

____

____

____

____

Daily Declaration Today I declare that my day will be _______________________

____

____

____

Future Focus My future self needs my current self to _______________________

______________________________ so that my future self will be able to ______

____

____

____

Purposeful Priority To ensure that I remain in alignment with my purpose, my number one priority today is to show up with a spirit of ____________________________

____

____

____

____

____

Recap & Re-do

Evening Gratitude

Night Vision

RENEW YOURSELF: DAILY THOUGHT WORK

Date______________

Memory Verse/Memory Quote ____

____

____

____

Morning Gratitude____

____

____

____

____

____

____

____

____

____

Daily Declaration Today I declare that my day will be ______________________

____

____

____

Future Focus My future self needs my current self to ______________________

________________________________ so that my future self will be able to ______

____

____

____

Purposeful Priority To ensure that I remain in alignment with my purpose, my number one priority today is to show up with a spirit of ______________________________

____

____

____

____

____

Recap & Re-do ____

____

____

____

____

____

____

____

____

____

Evening Gratitude ____

____

____

____

____

____

____

____

____

____

____

____

____

Night Vision ____

____

____

____

____

____

____

RENEW YOURSELF: WEEKLY REVIEW

Date ________________

BELIEF ASSESSMENT

Take this time to infer what your thoughts and gratitude say about your beliefs.

What do my thoughts show I believe in? ________________________________

____

____

____

____

What am I reading to develop, expand, or change my beliefs? ________________

____

____

____

____

____

MENTAL FOCUS ASSESSMENT

What things was I focused on this past week?

______________________	______________________
______________________	______________________
______________________	______________________
______________________	______________________
______________________	______________________
______________________	______________________
______________________	______________________
______________________	______________________

RENEW YOURSELF: WEEKLY REVIEW

Of these things, which are a necessary resource, task, or belief that I need to create the life I'm trying to build? Which are not?

NECESSARY	NOT NECESSARY
______________________	______________________
______________________	______________________
______________________	______________________
______________________	______________________
______________________	______________________
______________________	______________________

Why did I choose to focus on the things in the not necessary column? What am I going to do to make sure I don't waste time on these things going forward?____________

____

____

____

____

ACTIONS

What actions were in alignment with my beliefs and a result of my focus? ________

____

____

What actions were not in alignment with my beliefs?______________________

____

____

How can I make my actions align with my beliefs? ______________________

____

____

RENEW YOURSELF: DAILY THOUGHT WORK

Date______________

Memory Verse/Memory Quote ____

____

____

____

Morning Gratitude____

____

____

____

____

____

____

____

____

____

Daily Declaration Today I declare that my day will be ________________________

____

____

____

Future Focus My future self needs my current self to ________________________

________________________________ so that my future self will be able to ______

____

____

____

Purposeful Priority To ensure that I remain in alignment with my purpose, my number one priority today is to show up with a spirit of ____________________________

____

____

____

____

____

Recap & Re-do ___

Evening Gratitude ___

Night Vision ___

RENEW YOURSELF: DAILY THOUGHT WORK

Date______________

Memory Verse/Memory Quote ____
____
____
____

Morning Gratitude____
____
____
____
____
____
____
____
____
____

Daily Declaration Today I declare that my day will be ______________
____
____
____

Future Focus My future self needs my current self to _______________
___________________________ so that my future self will be able to ______
____
____
____

Purposeful Priority To ensure that I remain in alignment with my purpose, my number one priority today is to show up with a spirit of _________________
____
____
____
____
____

Recap & Re-do ______________________________

____

Evening Gratitude ______________________________

____

Night Vision ______________________________

____

RENEW YOURSELF: DAILY THOUGHT WORK

Date______________

Memory Verse/Memory Quote ____

____

____

____

Morning Gratitude____

____

____

____

____

____

____

____

____

____

Daily Declaration Today I declare that my day will be ______________________

____

____

____

Future Focus My future self needs my current self to ______________________

________________________________ so that my future self will be able to ______

____

____

____

Purposeful Priority To ensure that I remain in alignment with my purpose, my number one priority today is to show up with a spirit of ____________________________

____

____

____

____

____

Recap & Re-do ______________________________

Evening Gratitude ______________________________

Night Vision ______________________________

RENEW YOURSELF: DAILY THOUGHT WORK

Date______________

Memory Verse/Memory Quote ____

Morning Gratitude____

Daily Declaration Today I declare that my day will be ______________________

Future Focus My future self needs my current self to ________________________

___________________________________ so that my future self will be able to ______

Purposeful Priority To ensure that I remain in alignment with my purpose, my number one priority today is to show up with a spirit of ______________________________

Recap & Re-do ____

Evening Gratitude ____

Night Vision ____

RENEW YOURSELF: DAILY THOUGHT WORK

Date______________

Memory Verse/Memory Quote ____

Morning Gratitude____

Daily Declaration Today I declare that my day will be ______________________

Future Focus My future self needs my current self to _______________________
______________________________ so that my future self will be able to ______

Purposeful Priority To ensure that I remain in alignment with my purpose, my number one priority today is to show up with a spirit of _____________________________

Recap & Re-do

Evening Gratitude

Night Vision

RENEW YOURSELF: DAILY THOUGHT WORK

Date______________

Memory Verse/Memory Quote ____

____

____

____

Morning Gratitude____

____

____

____

____

____

____

____

____

____

Daily Declaration Today I declare that my day will be _______________________

____

____

____

Future Focus My future self needs my current self to ________________________
_________________________________ so that my future self will be able to ______

____

____

____

Purposeful Priority To ensure that I remain in alignment with my purpose, my number one priority today is to show up with a spirit of ______________________________

____

____

____

____

____

Recap & Re-do ____________________

Evening Gratitude ____________________

Night Vision ____________________

RENEW YOURSELF: DAILY THOUGHT WORK

Date______________

Memory Verse/Memory Quote ____

____

____

____

Morning Gratitude____

____

____

____

____

____

____

____

____

____

Daily Declaration Today I declare that my day will be _______________________

____

____

____

Future Focus My future self needs my current self to _____________________

_________________________________ so that my future self will be able to ______

____

____

____

Purposeful Priority To ensure that I remain in alignment with my purpose, my number one priority today is to show up with a spirit of ______________________________

____

____

____

____

____

Recap & Re-do ______

Evening Gratitude ______

Night Vision ______

RENEW YOURSELF: WEEKLY REVIEW

Date ________________

BELIEF ASSESSMENT

Take this time to infer what your thoughts and gratitude say about your beliefs.

What do my thoughts show I believe in? ________________________________

What am I reading to develop, expand, or change my beliefs? ____________

MENTAL FOCUS ASSESSMENT

What things was I focused on this past week?

RENEW YOURSELF: WEEKLY REVIEW

Of these things, which are a necessary resource, task, or belief that I need to create the life I'm trying to build? Which are not?

NECESSARY	NOT NECESSARY
______________________	______________________
______________________	______________________
______________________	______________________
______________________	______________________
______________________	______________________
______________________	______________________

Why did I choose to focus on the things in the not necessary column? What am I going to do to make sure I don't waste time on these things going forward?____________

____

____

____

____

ACTIONS

What actions were in alignment with my beliefs and a result of my focus? ________

____

____

What actions were not in alignment with my beliefs?____________________________

____

____

How can I make my actions align with my beliefs? ____________________________

____

____

RENEW YOURSELF: DAILY THOUGHT WORK

Date______________

Memory Verse/Memory Quote ____

____

____

____

Morning Gratitude____

____

____

____

____

____

____

____

____

____

Daily Declaration Today I declare that my day will be ______________________

____

____

____

Future Focus My future self needs my current self to ______________________

______________________________ so that my future self will be able to ______

____

____

____

Purposeful Priority To ensure that I remain in alignment with my purpose, my number one priority today is to show up with a spirit of ______________________

____

____

____

____

____

Recap & Re-do

Evening Gratitude

Night Vision

RENEW YOURSELF: DAILY THOUGHT WORK

Date______________

Memory Verse/Memory Quote ____

____

____

____

Morning Gratitude____

____

____

____

____

____

____

____

____

____

Daily Declaration Today I declare that my day will be ___________________

____

____

____

Future Focus My future self needs my current self to ___________________

______________________________ so that my future self will be able to ______

____

____

____

Purposeful Priority To ensure that I remain in alignment with my purpose, my number one priority today is to show up with a spirit of ____________________________

____

____

____

____

____

RENEW YOURSELF: DAILY THOUGHT WORK

Recap & Re-do

Evening Gratitude

Night Vision

RENEW YOURSELF: DAILY THOUGHT WORK

Date______________

Memory Verse/Memory Quote ____

Morning Gratitude____

Daily Declaration Today I declare that my day will be ______________________

Future Focus My future self needs my current self to _______________________

________________________________ so that my future self will be able to ______

Purposeful Priority To ensure that I remain in alignment with my purpose, my number one priority today is to show up with a spirit of ______________________________

Recap & Re-do ______________________________

Evening Gratitude ______________________________

Night Vision ______________________________

RENEW YOURSELF: DAILY THOUGHT WORK

Date_____________

Memory Verse/Memory Quote ______________________________________

____

____

____

Morning Gratitude____

____

____

____

____

____

____

____

____

____

Daily Declaration Today I declare that my day will be _______________________

____

____

____

Future Focus My future self needs my current self to ______________________

_____________________________ so that my future self will be able to ______

____

____

____

Purposeful Priority To ensure that I remain in alignment with my purpose, my number one priority today is to show up with a spirit of ___________________________

____

____

____

____

____

Recap & Re-do ________________________________

Evening Gratitude ________________________________

Night Vision ________________________________

RENEW YOURSELF: DAILY THOUGHT WORK

Date______________

Memory Verse/Memory Quote ____

____

____

____

Morning Gratitude____

____

____

____

____

____

____

____

____

____

Daily Declaration Today I declare that my day will be ______________________

____

____

____

Future Focus My future self needs my current self to ______________________

________________________________ so that my future self will be able to ______

____

____

____

Purposeful Priority To ensure that I remain in alignment with my purpose, my number one priority today is to show up with a spirit of ______________________________

____

____

____

____

____

Recap & Re-do ______________________________

Evening Gratitude ______________________________

Night Vision ______________________________

RENEW YOURSELF: DAILY THOUGHT WORK

Date____________

Memory Verse/Memory Quote ____________________________________

____

____

____

Morning Gratitude____

____

____

____

____

____

____

____

____

____

Daily Declaration Today I declare that my day will be ____________________

____

____

____

Future Focus My future self needs my current self to ____________________

____________________________ so that my future self will be able to ______

____

____

____

Purposeful Priority To ensure that I remain in alignment with my purpose, my number one priority today is to show up with a spirit of ________________________

____

____

____

____

____

Recap & Re-do ______________________________

Evening Gratitude ______________________________

Night Vision ______________________________

RENEW YOURSELF: DAILY THOUGHT WORK

Date______________

Memory Verse/Memory Quote ____

____

____

____

Morning Gratitude____

____

____

____

____

____

____

____

____

____

Daily Declaration Today I declare that my day will be ____________________

____

____

____

Future Focus My future self needs my current self to ______________________

______________________________ so that my future self will be able to ______

____

____

____

Purposeful Priority To ensure that I remain in alignment with my purpose, my number one priority today is to show up with a spirit of ____________________________

____

____

____

____

____

Recap & Re-do ______________________________

____

____

____

____

____

____

____

____

____

Evening Gratitude ______________________________

____

____

____

____

____

____

____

____

____

____

____

____

Night Vision ______________________________

____

____

____

____

____

____

RENEW YOURSELF: WEEKLY REVIEW

Date ________________

BELIEF ASSESSMENT

Take this time to infer what your thoughts and gratitude say about your beliefs.

What do my thoughts show I believe in? ________________________________

____

____

____

____

What am I reading to develop, expand, or change my beliefs? ________________

____

____

____

____

____

MENTAL FOCUS ASSESSMENT

What things was I focused on this past week?

______________________________ ______________________________

______________________________ ______________________________

______________________________ ______________________________

______________________________ ______________________________

______________________________ ______________________________

______________________________ ______________________________

______________________________ ______________________________

______________________________ ______________________________

______________________________ ______________________________

RENEW YOURSELF: WEEKLY REVIEW

Of these things, which are a necessary resource, task, or belief that I need to create the life I'm trying to build? Which are not?

NECESSARY	NOT NECESSARY
______________________	______________________
______________________	______________________
______________________	______________________
______________________	______________________
______________________	______________________

Why did I choose to focus on the things in the not necessary column? What am I going to do to make sure I don't waste time on these things going forward?___________

____

____

____

____

ACTIONS

What actions were in alignment with my beliefs and a result of my focus? ________

____

____

What actions were not in alignment with my beliefs?____________________

____

____

How can I make my actions align with my beliefs? ____________________

____

____

RENEW YOURSELF: DAILY THOUGHT WORK

Date______________

Memory Verse/Memory Quote ____

Morning Gratitude____

Daily Declaration Today I declare that my day will be _______________________

Future Focus My future self needs my current self to _______________________ ________________________________ so that my future self will be able to ______

Purposeful Priority To ensure that I remain in alignment with my purpose, my number one priority today is to show up with a spirit of ______________________________

Recap & Re-do ____

Evening Gratitude ____

Night Vision ____

RENEW YOURSELF: DAILY THOUGHT WORK

Date______________

Memory Verse/Memory Quote ____

____

____

____

Morning Gratitude____

____

____

____

____

____

____

____

____

____

Daily Declaration Today I declare that my day will be ______________________

____

____

____

Future Focus My future self needs my current self to ______________________

________________________________ so that my future self will be able to ______

____

____

____

Purposeful Priority To ensure that I remain in alignment with my purpose, my number one priority today is to show up with a spirit of ______________________________

____

____

____

____

____

Recap & Re-do ______________________________

Evening Gratitude ______________________________

Night Vision ______________________________

RENEW YOURSELF: DAILY THOUGHT WORK

Date______________

Memory Verse/Memory Quote ____

____

____

____

Morning Gratitude____

____

____

____

____

____

____

____

____

____

Daily Declaration Today I declare that my day will be ______________________

____

____

____

Future Focus My future self needs my current self to ______________________

______________________________ so that my future self will be able to ______

____

____

____

Purposeful Priority To ensure that I remain in alignment with my purpose, my number one priority today is to show up with a spirit of ____________________________

____

____

____

____

____

Recap & Re-do ______________________________

Evening Gratitude ______________________________

Night Vision ______________________________

RENEW YOURSELF: DAILY THOUGHT WORK

Date______________

Memory Verse/Memory Quote ____

Morning Gratitude____

Daily Declaration Today I declare that my day will be _______________________

Future Focus My future self needs my current self to ____ so that my future self will be able to ______

Purposeful Priority To ensure that I remain in alignment with my purpose, my number one priority today is to show up with a spirit of ________________________________

Recap & Re-do ____________________

Evening Gratitude ____________________

Night Vision ____________________

RENEW YOURSELF: DAILY THOUGHT WORK

Date______________

Memory Verse/Memory Quote ____

____

____

____

Morning Gratitude____

____

____

____

____

____

____

____

____

____

Daily Declaration Today I declare that my day will be _______________________

____

____

____

Future Focus My future self needs my current self to ______________________

________________________________ so that my future self will be able to ______

____

____

____

Purposeful Priority To ensure that I remain in alignment with my purpose, my number one priority today is to show up with a spirit of ______________________________

____

____

____

____

____

Recap & Re-do ____

Evening Gratitude ____

Night Vision ____

RENEW YOURSELF: DAILY THOUGHT WORK

Date______________

Memory Verse/Memory Quote ____

____

____

____

Morning Gratitude____

____

____

____

____

____

____

____

____

____

Daily Declaration Today I declare that my day will be ______________________

____

____

____

Future Focus My future self needs my current self to ______________________

________________________________ so that my future self will be able to ______

____

____

____

Purposeful Priority To ensure that I remain in alignment with my purpose, my number one priority today is to show up with a spirit of ______________________

____

____

____

____

____

Recap & Re-do ______________________________

____

____

____

____

____

____

____

____

____

Evening Gratitude ______________________________

____

____

____

____

____

____

____

____

____

____

____

____

Night Vision ______________________________

____

____

____

____

____

____

RENEW YOURSELF: DAILY THOUGHT WORK

Date______________

Memory Verse/Memory Quote ____

____

____

____

Morning Gratitude____

____

____

____

____

____

____

____

____

____

Daily Declaration Today I declare that my day will be ______________________

____

____

____

Future Focus My future self needs my current self to ______________________

________________________________ so that my future self will be able to ______

____

____

____

Purposeful Priority To ensure that I remain in alignment with my purpose, my number one priority today is to show up with a spirit of ______________________________

____

____

____

____

____

Recap & Re-do ______

Evening Gratitude ______

Night Vision ______

RENEW YOURSELF: WEEKLY REVIEW

Date ________________

BELIEF ASSESSMENT

Take this time to infer what your thoughts and gratitude say about your beliefs.

What do my thoughts show I believe in? ________________________________

____

____

____

____

What am I reading to develop, expand, or change my beliefs? ________________

____

____

____

____

____

MENTAL FOCUS ASSESSMENT

What things was I focused on this past week?

____________________________ ____________________________

____________________________ ____________________________

____________________________ ____________________________

____________________________ ____________________________

____________________________ ____________________________

____________________________ ____________________________

____________________________ ____________________________

____________________________ ____________________________

____________________________ ____________________________

RENEW YOURSELF: WEEKLY REVIEW

Of these things, which are a necessary resource, task, or belief that I need to create the life I'm trying to build? Which are not?

NECESSARY	NOT NECESSARY

Why did I choose to focus on the things in the not necessary column? What am I going to do to make sure I don't waste time on these things going forward?

ACTIONS

What actions were in alignment with my beliefs and a result of my focus?

What actions were not in alignment with my beliefs?

How can I make my actions align with my beliefs?

RENEW YOURSELF: DAILY THOUGHT WORK

Date______________

Memory Verse/Memory Quote ____

____

____

____

Morning Gratitude____

____

____

____

____

____

____

____

____

____

Daily Declaration Today I declare that my day will be ________________________

____

____

____

Future Focus My future self needs my current self to ______________________

________________________________ so that my future self will be able to ______

____

____

____

Purposeful Priority To ensure that I remain in alignment with my purpose, my number one priority today is to show up with a spirit of ______________________________

____

____

____

____

____

Recap & Re-do ______________________________

Evening Gratitude ______________________________

Night Vision ______________________________

RENEW YOURSELF: DAILY THOUGHT WORK

Date______________

Memory Verse/Memory Quote ____

____

____

____

Morning Gratitude____

____

____

____

____

____

____

____

____

____

Daily Declaration Today I declare that my day will be ______________________

____

____

____

Future Focus My future self needs my current self to ______________________

________________________________ so that my future self will be able to ______

____

____

____

Purposeful Priority To ensure that I remain in alignment with my purpose, my number one priority today is to show up with a spirit of ____________________________

____

____

____

____

____

Recap & Re-do ______________________________

Evening Gratitude ______________________________

Night Vision ______________________________

RENEW YOURSELF: DAILY THOUGHT WORK

Date______________

Memory Verse/Memory Quote ____

____

____

____

Morning Gratitude____

____

____

____

____

____

____

____

____

____

Daily Declaration Today I declare that my day will be _______________________

____

____

____

Future Focus My future self needs my current self to _______________________

______________________________ so that my future self will be able to ______

____

____

____

Purposeful Priority To ensure that I remain in alignment with my purpose, my number one priority today is to show up with a spirit of ____________________________

____

____

____

____

____

Recap & Re-do ____________________

Evening Gratitude ____________________

Night Vision ____________________

RENEW YOURSELF: DAILY THOUGHT WORK

Date______________

Memory Verse/Memory Quote ____

____

____

____

Morning Gratitude____

____

____

____

____

____

____

____

____

____

Daily Declaration Today I declare that my day will be _______________________

____

____

____

Future Focus My future self needs my current self to _______________________

________________________________ so that my future self will be able to ______

____

____

____

Purposeful Priority To ensure that I remain in alignment with my purpose, my number one priority today is to show up with a spirit of ______________________________

____

____

____

____

____

Recap & Re-do ______________________________

Evening Gratitude ______________________________

Night Vision ______________________________

RENEW YOURSELF: DAILY THOUGHT WORK

Date______________

Memory Verse/Memory Quote ______________________________________

Morning Gratitude____

Daily Declaration Today I declare that my day will be ______________________

Future Focus My future self needs my current self to ________________________ ______________________________ so that my future self will be able to ______

Purposeful Priority To ensure that I remain in alignment with my purpose, my number one priority today is to show up with a spirit of ____________________________

Recap & Re-do ______________________________

Evening Gratitude ______________________________

Night Vision ______________________________

RENEW YOURSELF: DAILY THOUGHT WORK

Date______________

Memory Verse/Memory Quote ____

____

____

____

Morning Gratitude____

____

____

____

____

____

____

____

____

____

Daily Declaration Today I declare that my day will be ______________________

____

____

____

Future Focus My future self needs my current self to ______________________

________________________________ so that my future self will be able to ______

____

____

____

Purposeful Priority To ensure that I remain in alignment with my purpose, my number one priority today is to show up with a spirit of ______________________________

____

____

____

____

____

Recap & Re-do ______

Evening Gratitude ______

Night Vision ______

RENEW YOURSELF: DAILY THOUGHT WORK

Date______________

Memory Verse/Memory Quote ____

____

____

____

Morning Gratitude____

____

____

____

____

____

____

____

____

____

Daily Declaration Today I declare that my day will be ______________________

____

____

____

Future Focus My future self needs my current self to ______________________

______________________________ so that my future self will be able to ______

____

____

____

Purposeful Priority To ensure that I remain in alignment with my purpose, my number one priority today is to show up with a spirit of ____________________________

____

____

____

____

____

Recap & Re-do ____

____

____

____

____

____

____

____

____

____

Evening Gratitude ____

____

____

____

____

____

____

____

____

____

____

____

____

Night Vision ____

____

____

____

____

____

____

RENEW YOURSELF: WEEKLY REVIEW

Date ________________

BELIEF ASSESSMENT

Take this time to infer what your thoughts and gratitude say about your beliefs.

What do my thoughts show I believe in? ________________________________

____

____

____

____

What am I reading to develop, expand, or change my beliefs? ________________

____

____

____

____

____

MENTAL FOCUS ASSESSMENT

What things was I focused on this past week?

____________________________ ____________________________

____________________________ ____________________________

____________________________ ____________________________

____________________________ ____________________________

____________________________ ____________________________

____________________________ ____________________________

____________________________ ____________________________

____________________________ ____________________________

____________________________ ____________________________

RENEW YOURSELF: WEEKLY REVIEW

Of these things, which are a necessary resource, task, or belief that I need to create the life I'm trying to build? Which are not?

NECESSARY	NOT NECESSARY
____________________________	____________________________
____________________________	____________________________
____________________________	____________________________
____________________________	____________________________
____________________________	____________________________
____________________________	____________________________

Why did I choose to focus on the things in the not necessary column? What am I going to do to make sure I don't waste time on these things going forward?____________

____

____

____

____

ACTIONS

What actions were in alignment with my beliefs and a result of my focus? ________

____

____

What actions were not in alignment with my beliefs?______________________

____

____

How can I make my actions align with my beliefs? ________________________

____

____

RENEW YOURSELF: DAILY THOUGHT WORK

Date______________

Memory Verse/Memory Quote ____

____

____

____

Morning Gratitude____

____

____

____

____

____

____

____

____

____

Daily Declaration Today I declare that my day will be ______________________

____

____

____

Future Focus My future self needs my current self to ______________________

________________________________ so that my future self will be able to ______

____

____

____

Purposeful Priority To ensure that I remain in alignment with my purpose, my number one priority today is to show up with a spirit of ______________________________

____

____

____

____

____

Recap & Re-do ____________________

Evening Gratitude ____________________

Night Vision ____________________

RENEW YOURSELF: DAILY THOUGHT WORK

Date______________

Memory Verse/Memory Quote ____

____

____

____

Morning Gratitude____

____

____

____

____

____

____

____

____

____

Daily Declaration Today I declare that my day will be _______________________

____

____

____

Future Focus My future self needs my current self to ________________________

_________________________________ so that my future self will be able to ______

____

____

____

Purposeful Priority To ensure that I remain in alignment with my purpose, my number one priority today is to show up with a spirit of _______________________________

____

____

____

____

____

Recap & Re-do ______________________________

Evening Gratitude ______________________________

Night Vision ______________________________

RENEW YOURSELF: DAILY THOUGHT WORK

Date______________

Memory Verse/Memory Quote ____

____

____

____

Morning Gratitude____

____

____

____

____

____

____

____

____

____

Daily Declaration Today I declare that my day will be ______________________

____

____

____

Future Focus My future self needs my current self to ______________________

________________________________ so that my future self will be able to ______

____

____

____

Purposeful Priority To ensure that I remain in alignment with my purpose, my number one priority today is to show up with a spirit of ______________________________

____

____

____

____

____

Recap & Re-do ______________________________

Evening Gratitude ______________________________

Night Vision ______________________________

RENEW YOURSELF: DAILY THOUGHT WORK

Date______________

Memory Verse/Memory Quote ____

____

____

____

Morning Gratitude____

____

____

____

____

____

____

____

____

____

Daily Declaration Today I declare that my day will be ______________________

____

____

____

Future Focus My future self needs my current self to ______________________

______________________________ so that my future self will be able to ______

____

____

____

Purposeful Priority To ensure that I remain in alignment with my purpose, my number one priority today is to show up with a spirit of ____________________________

____

____

____

____

____

Recap & Re-do ______

Evening Gratitude ______

Night Vision ______

RENEW YOURSELF: DAILY THOUGHT WORK

Date______________

Memory Verse/Memory Quote ______________________________________

____

____

____

Morning Gratitude____

____

____

____

____

____

____

____

____

____

Daily Declaration Today I declare that my day will be ______________________

____

____

____

Future Focus My future self needs my current self to ______________________

______________________________ so that my future self will be able to ______

____

____

____

Purposeful Priority To ensure that I remain in alignment with my purpose, my number one priority today is to show up with a spirit of ___________________________

____

____

____

____

____

Recap & Re-do ______________________________

Evening Gratitude ______________________________

Night Vision ______________________________

RENEW YOURSELF: DAILY THOUGHT WORK

Date______________

Memory Verse/Memory Quote ______________________________________
____
____
____

Morning Gratitude____
____
____
____
____
____
____
____
____
____

Daily Declaration Today I declare that my day will be ____________________
____
____
____

Future Focus My future self needs my current self to ____________________
______________________________ so that my future self will be able to ______
____
____
____

Purposeful Priority To ensure that I remain in alignment with my purpose, my number one priority today is to show up with a spirit of ____________________________
____
____
____
____
____

Recap & Re-do ______________________________

Evening Gratitude ______________________________

Night Vision ______________________________

RENEW YOURSELF: DAILY THOUGHT WORK

Date______________

Memory Verse/Memory Quote ____

____

____

____

Morning Gratitude____

____

____

____

____

____

____

____

____

____

Daily Declaration Today I declare that my day will be ______________________

____

____

____

Future Focus My future self needs my current self to ______________________

________________________________ so that my future self will be able to ______

____

____

____

Purposeful Priority To ensure that I remain in alignment with my purpose, my number one priority today is to show up with a spirit of ____________________________

____

____

____

____

____

Recap & Re-do ______________________________________

Evening Gratitude ______________________________________

Night Vision ______________________________________

RENEW YOURSELF: WEEKLY REVIEW

Date ________________

BELIEF ASSESSMENT

Take this time to infer what your thoughts and gratitude say about your beliefs.

What do my thoughts show I believe in? ________________

What am I reading to develop, expand, or change my beliefs? ________________

MENTAL FOCUS ASSESSMENT

What things was I focused on this past week?

RENEW YOURSELF: WEEKLY REVIEW

Of these things, which are a necessary resource, task, or belief that I need to create the life I'm trying to build? Which are not?

NECESSARY	NOT NECESSARY
______________________________	______________________________
______________________________	______________________________
______________________________	______________________________
______________________________	______________________________
______________________________	______________________________
______________________________	______________________________

Why did I choose to focus on the things in the not necessary column? What am I going to do to make sure I don't waste time on these things going forward?___________

____

____

____

____

ACTIONS

What actions were in alignment with my beliefs and a result of my focus? ________

____

____

What actions were not in alignment with my beliefs?________________________

____

____

How can I make my actions align with my beliefs? __________________________

____

____

RENEW YOURSELF: DAILY THOUGHT WORK

Date______________

Memory Verse/Memory Quote ____

____

____

____

Morning Gratitude____

____

____

____

____

____

____

____

____

____

Daily Declaration Today I declare that my day will be _______________________

____

____

____

Future Focus My future self needs my current self to _______________________

_______________________________ so that my future self will be able to ______

____

____

____

Purposeful Priority To ensure that I remain in alignment with my purpose, my number one priority today is to show up with a spirit of ____________________________

____

____

____

____

____

Recap & Re-do ____________________

Evening Gratitude ____________________

Night Vision ____________________

RENEW YOURSELF: DAILY THOUGHT WORK

Date______________

Memory Verse/Memory Quote ____

____

____

____

Morning Gratitude____

____

____

____

____

____

____

____

____

____

Daily Declaration Today I declare that my day will be ______________________

____

____

____

Future Focus My future self needs my current self to ______________________

________________________________ so that my future self will be able to ______

____

____

____

Purposeful Priority To ensure that I remain in alignment with my purpose, my number one priority today is to show up with a spirit of ______________________________

____

____

____

____

____

Recap & Re-do ______

Evening Gratitude ______

Night Vision ______

RENEW YOURSELF: DAILY THOUGHT WORK

Date____________

Memory Verse/Memory Quote ____

____

____

____

Morning Gratitude____

____

____

____

____

____

____

____

____

____

Daily Declaration Today I declare that my day will be ______________________

____

____

____

Future Focus My future self needs my current self to ______________________

______________________________ so that my future self will be able to ______

____

____

____

Purposeful Priority To ensure that I remain in alignment with my purpose, my number one priority today is to show up with a spirit of ____________________________

____

____

____

____

____

Recap & Re-do ____

Evening Gratitude ____

Night Vision ____

RENEW YOURSELF: DAILY THOUGHT WORK

Date______________

Memory Verse/Memory Quote ____

____

____

____

Morning Gratitude____

____

____

____

____

____

____

____

____

____

Daily Declaration Today I declare that my day will be ______________________

____

____

____

Future Focus My future self needs my current self to ______________________

________________________ so that my future self will be able to ______

____

____

____

Purposeful Priority To ensure that I remain in alignment with my purpose, my number one priority today is to show up with a spirit of ______________________

____

____

____

____

____

Recap & Re-do ______________________________

Evening Gratitude ______________________________

Night Vision ______________________________

RENEW YOURSELF: DAILY THOUGHT WORK

Date______________

Memory Verse/Memory Quote ____

____

____

____

Morning Gratitude____

____

____

____

____

____

____

____

____

____

Daily Declaration Today I declare that my day will be ______________________

____

____

____

Future Focus My future self needs my current self to ______________________

______________________________ so that my future self will be able to ______

____

____

____

Purposeful Priority To ensure that I remain in alignment with my purpose, my number one priority today is to show up with a spirit of ____________________________

____

____

____

____

____

Recap & Re-do

Evening Gratitude

Night Vision

RENEW YOURSELF: DAILY THOUGHT WORK

Date______________

Memory Verse/Memory Quote ______________________________

____

____

____

Morning Gratitude______________________________

____

____

____

____

____

____

____

____

____

Daily Declaration Today I declare that my day will be ______________________________

____

____

____

Future Focus My future self needs my current self to ______________________________

______________________________ so that my future self will be able to ______

____

____

____

Purposeful Priority To ensure that I remain in alignment with my purpose, my number one priority today is to show up with a spirit of ______________________________

____

____

____

____

____

Recap & Re-do ______________________________________

Evening Gratitude ______________________________________

Night Vision ______________________________________

RENEW YOURSELF: DAILY THOUGHT WORK

Date______________

Memory Verse/Memory Quote ____

____

____

____

Morning Gratitude____

____

____

____

____

____

____

____

____

____

Daily Declaration Today I declare that my day will be _______________________

____

____

____

Future Focus My future self needs my current self to _______________________

________________________________ so that my future self will be able to ______

____

____

____

Purposeful Priority To ensure that I remain in alignment with my purpose, my number one priority today is to show up with a spirit of ______________________________

____

____

____

____

____

Recap & Re-do ______________________________

Evening Gratitude ______________________________

Night Vision ______________________________

RENEW YOURSELF: WEEKLY REVIEW

Date ________________

BELIEF ASSESSMENT

Take this time to infer what your thoughts and gratitude say about your beliefs.

What do my thoughts show I believe in? ______________________________

____

____

____

____

What am I reading to develop, expand, or change my beliefs? ______________

____

____

____

____

____

MENTAL FOCUS ASSESSMENT

What things was I focused on this past week?

____________________________ ____________________________

____________________________ ____________________________

____________________________ ____________________________

____________________________ ____________________________

____________________________ ____________________________

____________________________ ____________________________

____________________________ ____________________________

____________________________ ____________________________

____________________________ ____________________________

RENEW YOURSELF: WEEKLY REVIEW

Of these things, which are a necessary resource, task, or belief that I need to create the life I'm trying to build? Which are not?

NECESSARY	NOT NECESSARY
______________________	______________________
______________________	______________________
______________________	______________________
______________________	______________________
______________________	______________________
______________________	______________________

Why did I choose to focus on the things in the not necessary column? What am I going to do to make sure I don't waste time on these things going forward?____________

____

____

____

____

ACTIONS

What actions were in alignment with my beliefs and a result of my focus? ________

____

____

What actions were not in alignment with my beliefs?____________________

____

____

How can I make my actions align with my beliefs? ____________________

____

____

RENEW YOURSELF: DAILY THOUGHT WORK

Date______________

Memory Verse/Memory Quote ____

____

____

____

Morning Gratitude____

____

____

____

____

____

____

____

____

____

Daily Declaration Today I declare that my day will be _______________________

____

____

____

Future Focus My future self needs my current self to _______________________

________________________________ so that my future self will be able to ______

____

____

____

Purposeful Priority To ensure that I remain in alignment with my purpose, my number one priority today is to show up with a spirit of ______________________________

____

____

____

____

____

Recap & Re-do ______________________________

Evening Gratitude ______________________________

Night Vision ______________________________

RENEW YOURSELF: DAILY THOUGHT WORK

Date______________

Memory Verse/Memory Quote ____

____

____

____

Morning Gratitude____

____

____

____

____

____

____

____

____

____

Daily Declaration Today I declare that my day will be _______________________

____

____

____

Future Focus My future self needs my current self to ______________________

_______________________________ so that my future self will be able to ______

____

____

____

Purposeful Priority To ensure that I remain in alignment with my purpose, my number one priority today is to show up with a spirit of ______________________________

____

____

____

____

____

Recap & Re-do ______________________________

Evening Gratitude ______________________________

Night Vision ______________________________

RENEW YOURSELF: DAILY THOUGHT WORK

Date_____________

Memory Verse/Memory Quote ______________________________________

____

____

____

Morning Gratitude____

____

____

____

____

____

____

____

____

____

Daily Declaration Today I declare that my day will be ______________________

____

____

____

Future Focus My future self needs my current self to ______________________

______________________________ so that my future self will be able to ______

____

____

____

Purposeful Priority To ensure that I remain in alignment with my purpose, my number one priority today is to show up with a spirit of ____________________________

____

____

____

____

____

Recap & Re-do ________________________________

Evening Gratitude ________________________________

Night Vision ________________________________

RENEW YOURSELF: DAILY THOUGHT WORK

Date_____________

Memory Verse/Memory Quote ____
____
____
____

Morning Gratitude____
____
____
____
____
____
____
____
____
____

Daily Declaration Today I declare that my day will be ______________________
____
____
____

Future Focus My future self needs my current self to ______________________
________________________________ so that my future self will be able to ______
____
____
____

Purposeful Priority To ensure that I remain in alignment with my purpose, my number one priority today is to show up with a spirit of ___________________________
____
____
____
____
____

Recap & Re-do ______________________________

Evening Gratitude ______________________________

Night Vision ______________________________

RENEW YOURSELF: DAILY THOUGHT WORK

Date______________

Memory Verse/Memory Quote ____

____

____

____

Morning Gratitude____

____

____

____

____

____

____

____

____

____

Daily Declaration Today I declare that my day will be ______________________

____

____

____

Future Focus My future self needs my current self to ____________________

______________________________ so that my future self will be able to ______

____

____

____

Purposeful Priority To ensure that I remain in alignment with my purpose, my number one priority today is to show up with a spirit of ____________________________

____

____

____

____

____

Recap & Re-do

Evening Gratitude

Night Vision

RENEW YOURSELF: DAILY THOUGHT WORK

Date______________

Memory Verse/Memory Quote ____

____

____

____

Morning Gratitude____

____

____

____

____

____

____

____

____

____

Daily Declaration Today I declare that my day will be _______________________

____

____

____

Future Focus My future self needs my current self to _______________________

________________________________ so that my future self will be able to ______

____

____

____

Purposeful Priority To ensure that I remain in alignment with my purpose, my number one priority today is to show up with a spirit of ______________________________

____

____

____

____

____

Recap & Re-do ____________________

Evening Gratitude ____________________

Night Vision ____________________

RENEW YOURSELF: DAILY THOUGHT WORK

Date_____________

Memory Verse/Memory Quote ______________________________________

____

____

____

Morning Gratitude______________________________________

____

____

____

____

____

____

____

____

____

Daily Declaration Today I declare that my day will be ____________________

____

____

____

Future Focus My future self needs my current self to ____________________

______________________________ so that my future self will be able to ______

____

____

____

Purposeful Priority To ensure that I remain in alignment with my purpose, my number one priority today is to show up with a spirit of ____________________

____

____

____

____

____

Recap & Re-do ______________________________

Evening Gratitude ______________________________

Night Vision ______________________________

RENEW YOURSELF: WEEKLY REVIEW

Date ________________

BELIEF ASSESSMENT

Take this time to infer what your thoughts and gratitude say about your beliefs.

What do my thoughts show I believe in? ______________________________

What am I reading to develop, expand, or change my beliefs? ________________

MENTAL FOCUS ASSESSMENT

What things was I focused on this past week?

RENEW YOURSELF: WEEKLY REVIEW

Of these things, which are a necessary resource, task, or belief that I need to create the life I'm trying to build? Which are not?

NECESSARY	NOT NECESSARY
____________________	____________________
____________________	____________________
____________________	____________________
____________________	____________________
____________________	____________________
____________________	____________________

Why did I choose to focus on the things in the not necessary column? What am I going to do to make sure I don't waste time on these things going forward?____________

____

____

____

____

ACTIONS

What actions were in alignment with my beliefs and a result of my focus? ________

____

____

What actions were not in alignment with my beliefs?____________________

____

____

How can I make my actions align with my beliefs? ____________________

____

____

RENEW YOURSELF: DAILY THOUGHT WORK

Date______________

Memory Verse/Memory Quote ____

____

____

____

Morning Gratitude____

____

____

____

____

____

____

____

____

____

Daily Declaration Today I declare that my day will be ______________________

____

____

____

Future Focus My future self needs my current self to ______________________

________________________________ so that my future self will be able to ______

____

____

____

Purposeful Priority To ensure that I remain in alignment with my purpose, my number one priority today is to show up with a spirit of ______________________________

____

____

____

____

____

Recap & Re-do ____

Evening Gratitude ____

Night Vision ____

RENEW YOURSELF: DAILY THOUGHT WORK

Date______________

Memory Verse/Memory Quote ____

____

____

____

Morning Gratitude____

____

____

____

____

____

____

____

____

____

Daily Declaration Today I declare that my day will be ____________________

____

____

____

Future Focus My future self needs my current self to ____________________

________________________________ so that my future self will be able to ______

____

____

____

Purposeful Priority To ensure that I remain in alignment with my purpose, my number one priority today is to show up with a spirit of ____________________

____

____

____

____

____

Recap & Re-do ______________________________

____

____

____

____

____

____

____

____

____

Evening Gratitude ______________________________

____

____

____

____

____

____

____

____

____

____

____

____

Night Vision ______________________________

____

____

____

____

____

____

RENEW YOURSELF: DAILY THOUGHT WORK

Date_____________

Memory Verse/Memory Quote ____

____

____

____

Morning Gratitude____

____

____

____

____

____

____

____

____

____

Daily Declaration Today I declare that my day will be ______________________

____

____

____

Future Focus My future self needs my current self to ______________________

________________________________ so that my future self will be able to ______

____

____

____

Purposeful Priority To ensure that I remain in alignment with my purpose, my number one priority today is to show up with a spirit of ___________________________

____

____

____

____

____

Recap & Re-do ______

Evening Gratitude ______

Night Vision ______

RENEW YOURSELF: DAILY THOUGHT WORK

Date______________

Memory Verse/Memory Quote ____

____

____

____

Morning Gratitude____

____

____

____

____

____

____

____

____

____

Daily Declaration Today I declare that my day will be ______________________

____

____

____

Future Focus My future self needs my current self to ______________________

________________________________ so that my future self will be able to ______

____

____

____

Purposeful Priority To ensure that I remain in alignment with my purpose, my number one priority today is to show up with a spirit of ______________________________

____

____

____

____

____

Recap & Re-do ______________________________

____
____
____
____
____
____
____
____
____

Evening Gratitude ______________________________

____
____
____
____
____
____
____
____
____
____
____
____

Night Vision ______________________________

____
____
____
____
____
____

RENEW YOURSELF: DAILY THOUGHT WORK

Date______________

Memory Verse/Memory Quote ____

____

____

____

Morning Gratitude____

____

____

____

____

____

____

____

____

____

Daily Declaration Today I declare that my day will be ____________________

____

____

____

Future Focus My future self needs my current self to ____________________

______________________________ so that my future self will be able to ______

____

____

____

Purposeful Priority To ensure that I remain in alignment with my purpose, my number one priority today is to show up with a spirit of ____________________________

____

____

____

____

____

Recap & Re-do

Evening Gratitude

Night Vision

RENEW YOURSELF: DAILY THOUGHT WORK

Date______________

Memory Verse/Memory Quote ____

____

____

____

Morning Gratitude____

____

____

____

____

____

____

____

____

____

Daily Declaration Today I declare that my day will be ________________________

____

____

____

Future Focus My future self needs my current self to ________________________

________________________________ so that my future self will be able to ______

____

____

____

Purposeful Priority To ensure that I remain in alignment with my purpose, my number one priority today is to show up with a spirit of ______________________________

____

____

____

____

____

Recap & Re-do ____

Evening Gratitude _____________________________________

Night Vision ____

RENEW YOURSELF: DAILY THOUGHT WORK

Date______________

Memory Verse/Memory Quote ____

____

____

____

Morning Gratitude____

____

____

____

____

____

____

____

____

____

Daily Declaration Today I declare that my day will be ______________________

____

____

____

Future Focus My future self needs my current self to ______________________

________________________________ so that my future self will be able to ______

____

____

____

Purposeful Priority To ensure that I remain in alignment with my purpose, my number one priority today is to show up with a spirit of ______________________________

____

____

____

____

____

Recap & Re-do ____________________

Evening Gratitude ____________________

Night Vision ____________________

RENEW YOURSELF: WEEKLY REVIEW

Date ________________

BELIEF ASSESSMENT

Take this time to infer what your thoughts and gratitude say about your beliefs.

What do my thoughts show I believe in? ______________________________

What am I reading to develop, expand, or change my beliefs? ________________

MENTAL FOCUS ASSESSMENT

What things was I focused on this past week?

RENEW YOURSELF: WEEKLY REVIEW

Of these things, which are a necessary resource, task, or belief that I need to create the life I'm trying to build? Which are not?

NECESSARY	NOT NECESSARY
____________________	____________________
____________________	____________________
____________________	____________________
____________________	____________________
____________________	____________________
____________________	____________________

Why did I choose to focus on the things in the not necessary column? What am I going to do to make sure I don't waste time on these things going forward?____________

____

____

____

____

ACTIONS

What actions were in alignment with my beliefs and a result of my focus? ________

____

____

What actions were not in alignment with my beliefs?_______________________

____

____

How can I make my actions align with my beliefs? _______________________

____

____

RENEW YOURSELF: DAILY THOUGHT WORK

Date______________

Memory Verse/Memory Quote ____

____

____

____

Morning Gratitude____

____

____

____

____

____

____

____

____

____

Daily Declaration Today I declare that my day will be ________________________

____

____

____

Future Focus My future self needs my current self to ________________________

_________________________________ so that my future self will be able to ______

____

____

____

Purposeful Priority To ensure that I remain in alignment with my purpose, my number one priority today is to show up with a spirit of ____________________________

____

____

____

____

____

Recap & Re-do

Evening Gratitude

Night Vision

RENEW YOURSELF: DAILY THOUGHT WORK

Date______________

Memory Verse/Memory Quote ____

____

____

____

Morning Gratitude____

____

____

____

____

____

____

____

____

____

Daily Declaration Today I declare that my day will be ______________________

____

____

____

Future Focus My future self needs my current self to ______________________

_______________________________ so that my future self will be able to ______

____

____

____

Purposeful Priority To ensure that I remain in alignment with my purpose, my number one priority today is to show up with a spirit of ____________________________

____

____

____

____

____

Recap & Re-do ______________________________

Evening Gratitude ______________________________

Night Vision ______________________________

RENEW YOURSELF: DAILY THOUGHT WORK

Date______________

Memory Verse/Memory Quote ____

____

____

____

Morning Gratitude____

____

____

____

____

____

____

____

____

____

Daily Declaration Today I declare that my day will be ______________________

____

____

____

Future Focus My future self needs my current self to ____________________

______________________________ so that my future self will be able to ______

____

____

____

Purposeful Priority To ensure that I remain in alignment with my purpose, my number one priority today is to show up with a spirit of ____________________________

____

____

____

____

____

Recap & Re-do ______________________________

____

____

____

____

____

____

____

____

____

Evening Gratitude ______________________________

____

____

____

____

____

____

____

____

____

____

____

____

Night Vision ______________________________

____

____

____

____

____

____

RENEW YOURSELF: DAILY THOUGHT WORK

Date______________

Memory Verse/Memory Quote ____

____

____

____

Morning Gratitude____

____

____

____

____

____

____

____

____

____

Daily Declaration Today I declare that my day will be ______________________

____

____

____

Future Focus My future self needs my current self to ______________________

________________________________ so that my future self will be able to ______

____

____

____

Purposeful Priority To ensure that I remain in alignment with my purpose, my number one priority today is to show up with a spirit of ______________________________

____

____

____

____

____

Recap & Re-do ______________________________

Evening Gratitude ______________________________

Night Vision ______________________________

RENEW YOURSELF: DAILY THOUGHT WORK

Date______________

Memory Verse/Memory Quote ____

____

____

____

Morning Gratitude____

____

____

____

____

____

____

____

____

____

Daily Declaration Today I declare that my day will be _______________________

____

____

____

Future Focus My future self needs my current self to _______________________

________________________________ so that my future self will be able to ______

____

____

____

Purposeful Priority To ensure that I remain in alignment with my purpose, my number one priority today is to show up with a spirit of ______________________________

____

____

____

____

____

Recap & Re-do ____

____

____

____

____

____

____

____

____

____

Evening Gratitude ____

____

____

____

____

____

____

____

____

____

____

____

____

Night Vision ____

____

____

____

____

____

____

RENEW YOURSELF: DAILY THOUGHT WORK

Date______________

Memory Verse/Memory Quote ____
____
____
____

Morning Gratitude____
____
____
____
____
____
____
____
____
____

Daily Declaration Today I declare that my day will be ______________________
____
____
____

Future Focus My future self needs my current self to ______________________
________________________________ so that my future self will be able to ______
____
____
____

Purposeful Priority To ensure that I remain in alignment with my purpose, my number one priority today is to show up with a spirit of ____________________________
____
____
____
____
____

Recap & Re-do ____

Evening Gratitude ____

Night Vision ____

RENEW YOURSELF: DAILY THOUGHT WORK

Date______________

Memory Verse/Memory Quote ____
____
____
____

Morning Gratitude____
____
____
____
____
____
____
____
____
____

Daily Declaration Today I declare that my day will be _______________________
____
____
____

Future Focus My future self needs my current self to ______________________
________________________________ so that my future self will be able
to ____
____
____

Purposeful Priority To ensure that I remain in alignment with my purpose, my number one priority today is to show up with a spirit of ________________
____
____
____
____
____

Recap & Re-do ______

Evening Gratitude ______

Night Vision ______

RENEW YOURSELF: WEEKLY REVIEW

Date ________________

BELIEF ASSESSMENT

Take this time to infer what your thoughts and gratitude say about your beliefs.

What do my thoughts show I believe in? ______________________________

____

____

____

____

What am I reading to develop, expand, or change my beliefs? ________________

____

____

____

____

____

MENTAL FOCUS ASSESSMENT

What things was I focused on this past week?

______________________ ______________________

______________________ ______________________

______________________ ______________________

______________________ ______________________

______________________ ______________________

______________________ ______________________

______________________ ______________________

______________________ ______________________

RENEW YOURSELF: WEEKLY REVIEW

Of these things, which are a necessary resource, task, or belief that I need to create the life I'm trying to build? Which are not?

NECESSARY	NOT NECESSARY
____________________	____________________
____________________	____________________
____________________	____________________
____________________	____________________
____________________	____________________
____________________	____________________
____________________	____________________

Why did I choose to focus on the things in the not necessary column? What am I going to do to make sure I don't waste time on these things going forward?____________

____

____

____

____

ACTIONS

What actions were in alignment with my beliefs and a result of my focus? ________

____

____

What actions were not in alignment with my beliefs?________________________

____

____

How can I make my actions align with my beliefs? __________________________

____

____

5
CONCLUSION

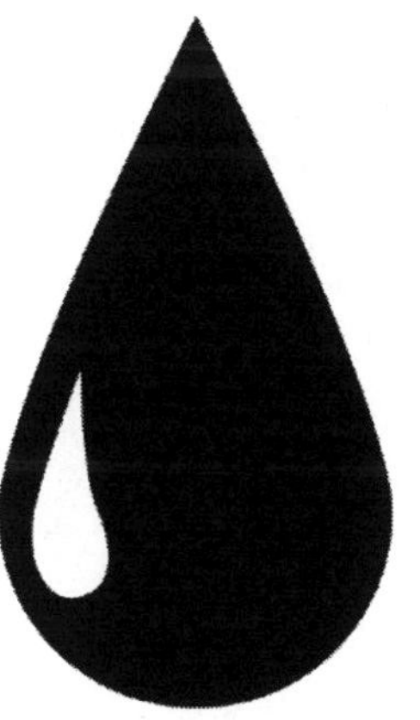

CONCLUSION: MY RESULTS

Before I started down this journey, everything I looked at was distorted. My view of myself, the world, and my future were so far off from the truth. I never knew that it was possible for me to enjoy waking up on a weekday without also loving my job. The power of knowing how to coral and redirect my thoughts throughout the day brings a peace that my mind could never comprehend before. I look forward to going to sleep now because I've traded restless nights for sleep that is so deep it feels like God Himself is holding me all night long. Thankfully, each step of the Mindsetting Method restored my perspective.

Rebuilding my belief in myself was an overwhelming process. Sometimes it still is. It's not that I had to learn to believe in myself. It's that I had to unlearn all the things everyone else wanted me to believe. I had to identify the difference between what is naturally part of me and what was poured into me. Then I had to decide if I wanted to keep any of the things that were instilled in me. All the books I read and experiences I've reflected on helped me realize that this is not only my challenge but, but something others face too.

Cleaning the environment of my mind required me to clean my home life also. I lowkey think that God knew I wouldn't do it on my own, so He brought single digit temperatures to the greater New York area and caused a pipe to burst and flood my apartment. Three days after my birthday! While I was still working on this book. Thankfully, I had put my Mindsetting notebook in my work bag that day. So, even though I was displaced from my apartment, I wasn't displaced in my mind. During the month I spent in the hotel, I continued to peacefully transform my mind. The time away from my home confirmed that the bulk of my work was in my mind, not my living space. Moving everything out of my apartment made purging easy. Having to step away from my home forced me to focus on myself. I used the daily thought work to analyze and redirect myself through my thoughts.

The daily thought work is literally my personal sunshine. I need it every day. Nothing bad happens when I miss a day, and thankfully, it only takes a couple of days for me feel the difference. Because stuff happens, there have been some days that I've missed. But, my toughest day since implementing The Mindsetting Method is much better than my best day before it. Looking back over my entries makes me very excited. I have already accomplished some of the things that I declared. It's good to be grateful for things before you can touch and feel them, but it's amazing to reflect on the fact that they did eventually come.

I now see the biggest sources of discomfort for what they really are—friction, not failure. Every person, situation, communication, or lack thereof, is a source of empowerment. They are opportunities for me to improve my approach or reaction, and everything else is merely friction that's sent to redirect me toward my purpose.

Below is a list of the specific changes I've seen in my life since I incorporated the Mindsetting Method:

- Overwhelming joy in the morning that continues to fuel me through the day
- Sleeping 6+ hours uninterrupted (no longer dreaming through late night tv)
- Controlling my thoughts; directing and redirecting them as necessary

- Significantly increasing my productivity and efficiency
- Making decisions easier, faster, and more accurately
- Waking up before my alarm clock on most days
- Staying focused at my job (this used to be hard because I don't love my job)
- Advocating for myself with calm power instead of tearful fear
- Acting with determination because my goals are now crystal clear
- Leveraging personal integrity to build internal drive to do exceptional work
- Completing dozens of important but outstanding commitments
- Learning to identify commitments that don't serve me well in advance
- Being strong enough to stop eating food I love but makes me feel bad
- Reducing my Fear of Missing Out (FOMO)
- Finding the good in every situation or encounter
- Thirsting for constructive criticism that causes reflection and growth

Some may look at these changes and conclude that The Mindsetting Method is a lot of work to do just to be able to get stuff done. But those of us who know the debilitating challenges of stagnation, depression, and a lack of self-worth see these for what they are—seismic shifts in the life of a person who has been paralyzed for years. These changes are the unseen foundational achievements that are necessary to meet the higher purpose of The Mindsetting Method: meaningful productivity.

Getting things done is worthless if you've done the wrong things. But worse, getting things done is incapacitating if you've done things that don't serve you well and or move you toward your goals. The things I listed above were all multi-year challenges I faced for the last decade. Incorporating the Mindsetting Method into my life has freed my mind from being concerned with these important (but seemingly miniscule) concerns. I no longer expend lots of mental energy managing these issues. Instead, I'm showing up daily having chosen a mindset that is consistently serving me well. It lets me focus on building the legacy of my dreams knowing that I have a foundation strong enough to withstand the storms that are sure to come.

Now I'm ready to take aim on my goals and live the life that I desire. I've dropped everyone else's expectations and forgiven myself for every mistake. Even the ones I continue to discover to this day. I'm literally on a warpath to my destiny. I'm ready, willing, and finally able to fight for myself. Not from a place of pity, but a place of transparent acknowledgement of my faults and anticipation of my growth.

The craziest part of it all is that if you look at my life too quickly you will miss all the signs of change. You have to look deeper into my hazel-amber colored eyes to see the glimmer of hope that now lives there. My smile lines run just a little deeper these days. My spirit is now whole and shines brighter than ever before.

No problem can be solved from the same level of consciousness that created it. ~Albert Einstein

CONCLUSION: YOUR NEXT STEPS

Continue to build your arsenal.

Treat your mind as an arsenal of information that you can reference whenever necessary. Like any master of their craft you must be an expert at using the tools that are available to you while also seeking to acquire new tools. The catch is knowing that your first craft is not working in a certain industry or building a specific skill—you are. To master your craft, you must first master yourself.

The process of mastering yourself is like a warrior building its arsenal of tools and techniques for fighting. To determine what other tools you need in your arsenal, you must increase your self-awareness. This is the point that often goes unnoticed. Everyone wants to be a fighter or a beast at what they do. But very few people want to do what it takes to get to that level.

Your arsenal is your personal curriculum of support, guidance, and perspective presented in an analyzed, synthesized, and organized way that you can consistently and constantly reference. You must become hungry enough to develop yourself into who you need to be to build the life that you want. The easiest way to do that is through reading and listening to audio books.

Unlike most podcasts, social media livestreams, and interviews, good books give you an in depth look at the mindset, energy, and feelings that were present during a journey. They don't just give you the highpoints and revelation. They take you on a journey. This is your chance to see yourself in them. Your chance to find similarities in how they were raised, decisions they have made, and most importantly, how they overcame.

For many people there was one good book, captivating story, or chance encounter that ignited their self-awareness journey. For me that book was *4-Hour Work Week* by Tim Ferris. In addition to making it super clear that the traditional work system wasn't necessary, it gave me a glimpse into the freelance, independent world of modern entrepreneurship. That book became a reference guide for how I would approach employment as I've slowly navigated my way out of corporate America. It is my hope and prayer that The Mindsetting Method will help you transform your mind and approach to thinking so you can exit corporate life much faster.

In addition to reading books, I strongly recommend that you review your daily thought work entries regularly. It's important that you reflect on who you were taught to be, who you really are, and who you are becoming. Reviewing the entries on the pages in the previous section will do just that. You can tell that your mind is transforming and developing a mindset that serves you when you are willing to be transparent about your journey. When you move from the safety of honesty to transparency you know you're growing.

As you're building your arsenal, please remember, it's not enough for you to learn and do the tasks to reach the specific goal. You have to want to become the version of yourself that can build the legacy you've envisioned. Consider all your resources, but always take responsibility for your final decision. If you maintain belief in yourself, demand that the environment of your mind stays clear and strong, and you consistently direct your thoughts toward your legacy, you will experience much more success faster than you can imagine.

I know that the metaphor that I used to introduce each chapter in this book has been about weapons and preparedness and tackling your challenges head on. There is however a brighter side to this journey. Since the challenging and pivotal time that caused me to write this book, I have learned so much about the joy and positivity that life can bring. And I want to encourage you that not only does life get better it gets brighter. Who you are today is not even a quarter of who you can be over the course of the rest of your life. So, I really urge you to take advantage of the knowledge that's in this book and every book that has ever been written. You deserve to learn more, to believe that you are worth more, and to live more.

GET CONTINUOUS SUPPORT

As I mentioned earlier, I wrote this book so you would know that you are not alone. But beyond just reading the book and doing the exercises within, I am available to continuously support you. Here's how you can maintain your growth momentum:

Join my private Facebook Group: This is a free resource community for employed entrepreneurs working to become full-time entrepreneurs. This community provides Mindsetting guidance and support to entrepreneurs who struggle with focusing their thoughts and actions on the "right" thing. Here you will get clarity, direction, and practical tips on how to fix your focus so you can finally stop wasting your 5-9pm time and accelerate your pace to become a full-time entrepreneur.

Invest in yourself & your business by joining Mindsetting to Millions. If you're building a business while working, this program is for you. The Mindsetting Method can get you to fulltime entrepreneurship much faster than any tool or program out there. This group coaching program will give you the safe environment to do each step of The Mindsetting Method while also learning from the transformation of others. An understanding and supportive but honestly critical environment is exactly what you need to get you to your next level of growth. Your business growth will never outpace your mindset. So, get started today!

Visit me at StartMindsetting.com and take the Sow What Matters Pledge. Remind yourself of the importance of sowing seeds of greatness. Stop sowing seeds of likes on Instagram, video views on Facebook, more Clients on your email list. You need to begin to develop the ability to isolate your focus. And to relentlessly pursue that goal with the knowledge that it won't be easy, and it won't happen the first time out the gate. Don't focus on tasks. Focus on understanding your methods, your approach, your perspective and confirming that they are all guiding you toward your goal.

CONCLUSION: ABOUT THE AUTHOR

Nia K. N. Jackson is a speaker, consultant, and Mindsetting™ coach. She is the creator of The Mindsetting Method and the founder of Beyond Encouragement (BE), a transformational education company.

Nia provides virtual coaching to working female business owners of color seeking to become full-time entrepreneurs. Primarily through virtual coaching, she teaches her clients how to shift their mindset from employee to entrepreneur. She helps them discover and leverage the mindset that best serves them and their business. Nia challenges her clients to remember that their business success will never outpace their self-awareness and personal development.

Nia is a graduate of Villanova University. She received her International MBA from Pepperdine University and her Juris Doctor from Hofstra School of Law. She is an attorney admitted to the New York State Bar. Nia believes that home is where the heart is, and her heart will always be in Houston, TX where she was born, New Orleans, LA where she grew up, and Long Island, NY where she currently resides.

Find Nia on social:

StartMindsetting.com **@MsNiaJackson** **@MindsettingMethod**

ACKNOWLEDGEMENTS

I thank God for my life. I also thank Him for sending me people that have been wonderful stewards of His Word in my life. Thank you for trusting me enough to show them love and kindness in return.

To my Top 5, you were and continue to be phenomenal sources of wisdom, love, and perseverance. Grandmother, Momma, Jack, Daddy, and Massa, your collective efforts made my life and this book possible. I'm eternally grateful to each of you.

To my sister and brother, y'all are the living examples of unconditional love. No matter how near or far we are from each other, I can always feel your love.

Triple S. a.k.a. my Stedman, I love this journey we are traveling. Thank you for letting me share these years with you. I'm eternally grateful for your patience, grace, and honesty.

Casey and Darby, your detailed critiques of each draft were nothing short of God's handiwork. I'm so blessed to call you both friends. I'm thankful that God knows when to introduce and re-introduce people into my life. I can't wait to see what the future holds for us!

No one travels the journey of life alone. I'm immensely grateful for everyone who has ever prayed for me and encouraged me to achieve my dreams. Each time I pause, your words revive me and push me to keep walking and working toward my legacy.

Made in the USA
Lexington, KY
22 August 2019